THE KNOWING PLACE DEVOTIONAL

Juanita Renee Burgess

Table Of Contents

Introduction

That hollow feeling in your chest during Sunday morning worship isn't doubt creeping in. It's not spiritual weakness or a sign that your faith is failing. That restless ache, that quiet hunger gnawing at your soul while everyone around you seems satisfied with surface-level Christianity, is actually God Himself calling you into something deeper, richer, and more real than anything you've experienced before.

You've been sitting in church services for months, maybe years, listening to sermons about God's love and reading Bible verses that talk about His presence, but something inside you keeps whispering that there has to be more. You watch other believers talk about hearing God's voice and experiencing His presence, and you wonder what's wrong with you because your prayers feel like they hit the ceiling and bounce back down.

Nothing is wrong with you.

You're ready for the next level of spiritual maturity. You're ready to move beyond knowing about Jesus to actually knowing Him personally, intimately, and daily. You're ready to stop living on borrowed faith and start building your own unshakeable relationship with the living

God who created you specifically to commune with Him.

This devotional isn't a feel-good collection of inspirational thoughts. This is a 60-day intensive devotional that will strategically teach you how to recognize God's voice, sense His presence, and build the kind of intimate relationship with Jesus that transforms everything about how you live, think, and respond to life's challenges.

Your Spiritual Hunger Is Actually God's Invitation

Every time you sit in church feeling spiritually empty while the person next to you raises their hands in worship, God is stirring something inside you. Every time you read a Bible verse and think "this sounds nice, but I don't feel it," the Holy Spirit is preparing you for a deeper encounter. Every time you pray and wonder if God hears you, He's drawing you closer to a place where you'll know beyond any doubt that He not only hears you but speaks back.

Your spiritual dissatisfaction is not a problem to solve. It's an invitation to accept. God plants holy dissatisfaction in the hearts of believers who are ready to graduate from spiritual elementary school into mature, intimate relationship with Him. He creates that restless ache in people who have tasted enough of His goodness to know there's more available but haven't yet learned how to access the fullness of His presence.

Think about physical hunger for a moment. When your stomach growls, it's not telling you something is wrong with your digestive system. It's telling you that your body needs food and knows where to find it. Spiritual hunger works the same way. That ache in your soul isn't a sign that you're spiritually broken or that God is distant from you.

It's your spirit recognizing that you were created for intimate communion with your Creator, and it won't be satisfied with anything less than the real thing. Your spirit knows the difference between reading about God's love and experiencing it personally. Your spirit can tell the difference between hearing someone else's testimony about God's faithfulness and having your own encounters with His goodness.

The reason Sunday services leave you feeling empty isn't because there's anything wrong with corporate worship or church community. Corporate worship is beautiful and necessary. The problem is that you've outgrown spiritual milk and your soul is crying out for solid food. You need more than weekly encouragement. You need daily encounter.

You need to learn how to meet with God personally, consistently, and intimately every single day until His presence becomes as real to you as the air you breathe. You need to develop the spiritual skills that allow you to hear His voice clearly, sense His guidance confidently, and rest in His love completely regardless of what's happening in your circumstances.

God has been preparing you for this season. Every disappointment with shallow Christianity, every moment of feeling spiritually hungry while others seemed satisfied, every prayer that felt unanswered has been God's way of creating space in your heart for something much better than what you've been settling for.

He wants to teach you how to live from a place of spiritual fullness instead of spiritual emptiness. He wants to show you how to commune with Him so naturally and consistently that you never again have to wonder if He's listening or if He cares about the details of your daily life.

Why This Devotional Changes Everything

Most devotionals give you a Bible verse, a short inspirational thought, and a prayer to recite. This devotional teaches you how to actually commune with the living God who inspired those verses. Most devotionals tell you what other people have experienced with God. This devotional creates daily opportunities for you to have your own encounters with His presence.

On this devotional journey, you're going to learn practical, specific skills that mature believers use to maintain intimate relationship with Jesus. You're going to discover how to recognize when God is speaking to your spirit, how to distinguish His voice from your own thoughts and emotions, and how to respond to His leading with confidence and obedience.

Each chapter includes carefully selected scripture, which provides deeper insight into the original meaning of biblical text and helps you understand the full richness of what God is communicating. You'll learn how to read scripture not just for information but for personal encounter, allowing the Holy Spirit to speak directly to your heart through His written word.

But reading scripture is only the beginning. Each chapter devotion includes guided reflection questions designed to help you process what God is saying to you personally through that day's passage. These aren't generic questions that could apply to anyone. These are specific, targeted questions that help you identify how God wants to work in your specific circumstances, relationships, and spiritual growth areas.

Then comes the most important part: practical spiritual exercises that create space for God to speak back to you. You'll learn how to pray conversationally instead of just talking at God. You'll discover how to listen for His voice and recognize when He's responding to your prayers. You'll develop the spiritual sensitivity that allows you to sense His presence throughout your day, not just during your morning devotion time.

This devotional will teach you how to carry the presence of God with you into every conversation, every decision, every challenge, and every opportunity you face. You'll learn how to live from a place of constant communion with Jesus instead of trying to survive on the spiritual energy you get from Sunday services.

Along the way, you'll notice that your prayers feel different. Instead of hoping God hears you, you'll know He's listening because you've learned to recognize the subtle ways He responds. As you continue, you'll start making decisions with confidence because you've developed the spiritual discernment that comes from regular communion with the Holy Spirit.

By the end, you'll have built the foundation for a lifetime of intimate relationship with Jesus that can't be shaken by difficult circumstances, disappointing people, or spiritual dry seasons. You'll have moved from hoping God loves you to knowing you are His beloved. You'll have graduated from wondering if God has a plan for your life to walking confidently in His daily guidance.

Your Journey from Believing to Knowing

There's a massive difference between believing God exists and actually knowing Him personally. Believing is intellectual agreement with biblical truth. Knowing is intimate, personal, experiential relationship with the living God who wants to be involved in every detail of your daily life.

You can believe that God loves you while still feeling insecure about your worth and value. But when you know God loves you because you've experienced His love personally and repeatedly, that knowledge becomes unshakeable. You can believe that God has a plan for your life while still feeling anxious about the future. But when you know God's voice and have learned to follow His daily guidance, you can face uncertainty with peace and confidence.

This devotional journey is specifically designed to move you from the realm of believing into the realm of knowing. Each chapter builds on the previous chapter, systematically developing your spiritual sensitivity and your ability to commune with God intimately and consistently.

Chapter one focuses on learning to recognize God's voice. You'll discover the different ways God speaks to His children and learn to distinguish His voice from your own thoughts, emotions, and the opinions of other people. You'll practice listening prayer and learn how to create space for God to respond when you talk to Him.

Chapter two teaches you how to sense God's presence throughout your day. You'll learn practical techniques for maintaining awareness of His nearness even during busy, stressful, or mundane activities. You'll discover how to invite God into your work, your relationships, and your decision-making process.

Chapters three and four focus on building consistent intimacy with Jesus through scripture meditation and conversational prayer. You'll move beyond reading Bible verses for information and learn how to allow the Holy Spirit to speak to you personally through His written word. You'll develop the habit of ongoing dialogue with God that makes prayer feel natural and conversational rather than formal and one-sided.

The middle chapters of this devotional teach you how to apply what you're learning in practical ways. You'll discover how to seek God's guidance for specific decisions, how to pray effectively for other people, and how to maintain your connection with God during difficult or stressful seasons.

The final chapters focus on establishing these practices as permanent lifestyle changes rather than temporary spiritual disciplines. You'll learn how to continue growing in intimacy with God and how to help other believers develop their own personal relationships with Jesus.

Each chapter's devotion includes specific, actionable steps you can take immediately. You won't find vague suggestions like "spend more time with God" or "pray more often." Instead, you'll get clear instructions like "Set a timer for five minutes and ask God this specific question, then sit quietly and write down whatever comes to mind" or "Read this passage three times slowly, then ask the Holy Spirit to show you one specific way to apply it today."

This devotional respects your intelligence and your spiritual hunger. It doesn't talk down to you or assume you need basic explanations of elementary Christian concepts. It meets you where you are as a believer who already knows the fundamentals of faith and is ready to build something deeper, stronger, and more intimate with the

God who created you for relationship with Himself.

By the end of this devotional, you'll have developed the spiritual skills and habits that allow mature believers to live in constant communion with Jesus. You'll have your own personal history of encounters with God's presence, your own collection of memories where you clearly heard His voice and followed His guidance, and your own unshakeable confidence in His love for you.

You'll never again have to wonder if God cares about your daily concerns or if He's actively involved in your life. You'll know because you'll have learned to recognize His involvement, His guidance, and His presence as normal parts of your everyday experience.

Chapter 1 | Breaking Free from Surface Faith

Blessed [joyful, nourished by God's goodness] are those who hunger and thirst for righteousness [those who actively seek right standing with God], for they will be [completely] satisfied. Matthew 5:6 AMP

Surface faith feels safe because it asks so little of you, but it leaves your soul starving for the very thing God created you to experience. You show up to church, sing the songs, listen to sermons, and check all the boxes that good Christians are supposed to check, yet something deep inside you remains untouched, unfed, and unsatisfied. That gnawing emptiness you feel after every Sunday service isn't a sign that you're doing Christianity wrong.

It's proof that you're ready for Christianity done right.

The traditional church experience was never meant to be your primary source of spiritual nourishment any more than a weekly family dinner was meant to be your only meal. Church is meant to be a celebration of the intimate relationship you're already building with God throughout the week, not a substitute for that relationship. When you try to survive spiritually on Sunday services alone, you're essentially trying to live on one meal per week while wondering why you feel weak and hungry.

Your spirit knows the difference between performance and presence, between religious activity and authentic encounter, between hearing about God and hearing from God. That's why you can sit through powerful worship services and inspiring sermons while feeling spiritually empty. That's why you can participate in all the right Christian activities while still feeling like something crucial is missing from your faith experience.

What's missing isn't more church involvement or better Bible study materials or stronger commitment to religious disciplines. What's missing is personal, intimate, daily communion with the living God who wants to be actively involved in every detail of your life. What's missing is the kind of relationship with Jesus that makes His presence feel as real and consistent as your next heartbeat.

Why Church Culture Leaves You Spiritually Hungry

Church culture operates on a performance model that

treats spiritual growth like a group activity, but authentic relationship with God happens in the secret place of personal encounter. Corporate worship services are designed to inspire and encourage large groups of people with varying levels of spiritual maturity, which means they naturally aim for the middle ground of spiritual experience rather than the deep end where your soul wants to swim.

When you're spiritually hungry for intimate encounter with God, sitting through another sermon about God's love feels like reading a restaurant menu when what you actually need is a meal. The information might be accurate and even beautifully presented, but it doesn't satisfy the deep hunger in your spirit for personal experience of that love. You need to taste and see that the Lord is good, not just hear someone else describe how good He tastes.

Most church programming focuses on teaching you about God rather than teaching you how to commune with God. You learn biblical facts, theological concepts, and moral principles, but you don't learn the practical skills that allow you to recognize God's voice, sense His presence, or respond to His daily guidance. You graduate from years of church attendance knowing a lot about prayer but never having learned how to pray conversationally. You can quote verses about God's faithfulness but you've never developed your own personal history of experiencing His faithfulness in your specific circumstances.

This creates a generation of believers who are biblically informed but spiritually malnourished, people who can discuss doctrine but struggle to discern God's will, Christians who know all the right answers but don't know how to ask God the right questions. You end up feeling like a spiritual outsider even within your own church community because everyone seems satisfied with a level of spiritual experience that leaves you feeling empty and restless.

The problem isn't that church is bad or that corporate worship is unnecessary. The problem is that church culture has accidentally trained you to think that showing up to religious events is the same thing as building intimate relationship with Jesus. It's like thinking that attending cooking classes makes you a chef without ever actually preparing a meal yourself. You can learn all the techniques and understand all the principles, but until you get in the kitchen and start cooking, you'll never develop the skills that come from hands-on experience.

Church services give you the recipes for spiritual growth, but they can't do the actual cooking for you. That happens in your personal time with God, in the quiet moments when you learn to recognize His voice, in the daily decisions where you practice following His guidance, in the private conversations where you discover that He actually talks back when you learn how to listen.

Traditional church programming also operates on a one-size-fits-all approach that doesn't account for the fact that God speaks to different people in different ways. Some people sense God's presence most clearly through worship music, others through scripture meditation, others through quiet contemplation, and still others through serving other people. But church services typically offer the same spiritual diet to everyone regardless of how God has uniquely wired them to connect with His presence.

When your spiritual appetite doesn't match what's being served on Sunday morning, you can start to wonder if something is wrong with you spiritually. You might think you're not worshipful enough because you don't get emotional during the music, or not spiritual enough because the sermon doesn't move you the way it seems to move other people. The truth is that God designed you with a unique spiritual personality that connects with His presence in specific ways, and you need to discover and develop those ways through personal experimentation and practice.

Church culture also tends to emphasize spiritual

consumption over spiritual contribution. You come to receive a blessing, hear a word from God, or get your spiritual tank filled, but you're not taught how to generate your own spiritual momentum through personal communion with God. This creates a dependency on external spiritual sources that leaves you feeling empty and directionless between Sundays.

When your primary spiritual input comes from other people's encounters with God rather than your own personal experiences, your faith becomes secondhand instead of firsthand. You're living on borrowed spiritual energy instead of generating your own through direct relationship with Jesus. This is why even the most inspiring church services leave you feeling spiritually hungry within a few days. You're trying to survive on someone else's spiritual meal instead of learning how to feed yourself through personal communion with God.

Recognizing Your Holy Dissatisfaction

That restless feeling you experience during church services isn't spiritual immaturity. It's spiritual readiness. God plants holy dissatisfaction in the hearts of believers who are ready to graduate from spiritual elementary school into mature, intimate relationship with Him. When you feel bored during sermons that used to inspire you, when worship songs that once moved you now feel empty, when Bible studies that used to challenge you now seem shallow, God is stirring something deeper in your spirit.

Your dissatisfaction with surface-level Christianity is actually evidence that the Holy Spirit is calling you into something richer, deeper, and more personally transformative than what you've been experiencing. It's proof that your spiritual appetite has grown beyond what traditional church programming can satisfy. Just like a teenager eventually outgrows children's books and needs more complex literature to engage their developing mind, your spirit has outgrown spiritual milk and is crying out for solid food.

This holy dissatisfaction often comes with feelings of guilt or confusion because church culture teaches us that good Christians should be satisfied with regular church attendance and basic spiritual disciplines. When you find yourself wanting more than what's offered in typical Christian programming, you might wonder if you're being prideful, ungrateful, or spiritually rebellious. You might think something is wrong with your heart because you're no longer content with the level of spiritual experience that seems to satisfy other believers.

Nothing is wrong with your heart. Everything is right

with your spiritual appetite.

God creates spiritual hunger in people who are ready to move beyond knowing about Him into actually knowing Him personally. He stirs up holy dissatisfaction in believers who have tasted enough of His goodness to recognize that there's more available but haven't yet learned how to access the fullness of His presence. Your restlessness with shallow Christianity is God's invitation to go deeper, not a sign that you need to try harder to be satisfied with less.

This season of spiritual dissatisfaction is actually a gift from God, even though it feels uncomfortable and sometimes isolating. It's His way of creating space in your heart for something much better than what you've been settling for. Just like physical hunger motivates you to seek food, spiritual hunger motivates you to seek more intimate communion with your Creator. Without that hunger, you might remain content with surface-level faith for the rest of your life, never discovering the incredible intimacy that God wants to share with you.

Your holy dissatisfaction also serves as protection against spiritual complacency. It keeps you from settling for religious routine instead of authentic relationship. It prevents you from becoming satisfied with knowing about God instead of actually knowing Him. It creates the internal motivation you need to do the hard work of building genuine intimacy with Jesus rather than just going through the motions of Christian living.

Many mature believers go through a season where they feel spiritually homeless even within their own church communities. They love Jesus and want to grow in their faith, but they feel disconnected from the typical expressions of Christianity that used to satisfy them. They find themselves craving deeper spiritual conversation than what happens in most small groups. They want to learn practical skills for hearing God's voice rather than just discussing Bible verses. They're hungry for personal encounter with God's presence rather than just hearing about other people's spiritual experiences.

If this describes your current spiritual state, you're not backsliding or losing your faith. You're not being critical or hard to please. You're experiencing the natural progression of spiritual maturity that happens when God prepares someone for deeper levels of intimacy with Him. Your dissatisfaction with shallow Christianity is evidence that the Holy Spirit is drawing you into the kind of personal relationship with Jesus that most believers never discover because they remain satisfied with surface-level faith.

This holy dissatisfaction will continue until you learn how to satisfy your spiritual hunger through direct, personal communion with God rather than trying to survive on the spiritual energy you get from corporate worship services. It will keep stirring in your heart until you develop the skills that allow you to recognize God's voice, sense His presence, and respond to His guidance as natural parts of your daily experience.

The goal isn't to eliminate your spiritual hunger but to learn how to feed it properly through intimate relationship with Jesus. God wants you to remain spiritually hungry because spiritual hunger keeps you seeking Him, keeps you growing, and keeps you open to deeper levels of His presence and truth. But He also wants you to know how to satisfy that hunger through personal encounter rather than leaving church services feeling empty and frustrated.

Permission to Pursue Authentic Relationship

You have God's full permission to abandon comfortable religious routines that no longer feed your soul and pursue the kind of authentic relationship with Jesus that your spirit is craving. You don't need approval from church leadership, agreement from other believers, or validation from Christian friends to begin building the intimate communion with God that He created you to experience. Your spiritual hunger is authorization enough.

God is not offended when you outgrow surface-level Christianity any more than parents are offended when their children outgrow elementary education and need more advanced learning opportunities. He's not disappointed in you for wanting more than what traditional church programming offers. He's the one who planted that desire for deeper intimacy in your heart in the first place. He's been preparing you for this season of spiritual growth by creating holy dissatisfaction with anything less than genuine encounter with His presence.

Many believers feel guilty about stepping away from religious activities that no longer serve their spiritual growth because church culture often equates faithfulness with attendance and commitment with participation in programs. But faithfulness to God means pursuing the kind of relationship with Him that actually transforms your heart, not just maintaining religious habits that make other people comfortable. Commitment to Jesus means doing whatever it takes to know Him personally and intimately, even if that means disappointing people who expect you to remain satisfied with shallow Christianity.

You have permission to skip church events that feel spiritually empty so you can spend that time in personal communion with God. You have permission to leave Bible studies that focus on information rather than transformation so you can pursue spiritual practices that actually deepen your intimacy with Jesus. You have permission to step away from Christian activities that drain your spiritual energy so you can invest that energy in learning how to commune with God directly.

This doesn't mean you should abandon Christian community or isolate yourself from other believers. Healthy Christian community is essential for spiritual growth and accountability. But it does mean you should prioritize building your personal relationship with God over maintaining religious appearances or meeting other people's expectations about how committed Christians should behave.

God wants you to become spiritually self-feeding rather than dependent on external sources for your spiritual nourishment. He wants you to learn how to commune with Him so naturally and consistently that you come to church services to celebrate the relationship you're already building with Him throughout the week, not to get your weekly spiritual fix. He wants you to develop such intimate knowledge of His voice and His ways that you can discern His will confidently and follow His guidance obediently regardless of what other people think you should do.

This kind of spiritual maturity requires you to take responsibility for your own spiritual growth rather than expecting church programming to do the work for you. It means learning to recognize what feeds your soul and what leaves you spiritually empty, then making choices that prioritize your spiritual health over social expectations. It means being willing to disappoint people who want you to remain at their level of spiritual experience so you can pursue the level of intimacy with God that your heart is seeking.

You also have permission to pursue spiritual practices that feel authentic to you even if they're different from what other believers find helpful. Some people connect with God most deeply through extended times of worship music. Others sense His presence most clearly in complete silence. Some hear His voice through scripture meditation while others recognize His guidance through circumstances and inner peace. God designed you with a unique spiritual personality, and He wants you to discover the specific ways He's wired you to commune with His presence.

Traditional church programming tends to offer the

same spiritual diet to everyone, but God speaks to different people in different ways. Your job is to discover how He speaks to you specifically, then develop those communication channels through consistent practice. You have permission to experiment with different spiritual disciplines until you find the ones that deepen your intimacy with Jesus rather than just fulfilling religious obligations.

You have permission to ask God hard questions about faith, life, and His will for your specific circumstances. You have permission to bring your doubts, fears, and confusion directly to Him rather than pretending you have everything figured out. You have permission to be honest with God about your spiritual struggles, your disappointments with church culture, and your hunger for more authentic relationship with Him.

God is not fragile. He can handle your questions, your frustrations, and your desire for something deeper than surface-level Christianity. In fact, He's been waiting for you to bring these things to Him directly rather than trying to solve them through religious activity or spiritual performance. Your willingness to be authentic with God about your spiritual needs is the beginning of the kind of honest, intimate relationship that He's been wanting to build with you.

Preparing Your Heart for Deeper Encounter

Building authentic intimacy with God requires the same intentionality and preparation that any meaningful relationship demands, but most believers have never been taught how to create the internal conditions that allow them to recognize God's presence and respond to His voice. Your heart is like soil that needs specific preparation before it can receive and nurture the seeds of deeper spiritual experience that God wants to plant in your life.

The first step in preparing your heart for deeper encounter is creating space for God to actually speak back when you pray. Most people pray by talking at God rather than talking with God because they've never learned how to listen for His response. They present their requests, share their concerns, and express their gratitude, but they don't pause long enough to hear if He has anything to say back to them. This turns prayer into a monologue instead of a conversation.

Start building space for God's response into every prayer time by setting aside at least five minutes after you finish talking to simply sit quietly and listen. Don't expect to hear an audible voice or receive dramatic revelations. God usually speaks through gentle impressions, sudden insights, scripture verses that come to mind, or a sense of peace about specific decisions. Learn to pay attention to what thoughts, ideas, or emotions surface during these quiet listening times.

Write down whatever comes to mind during your listening times, even if it seems insignificant or you're not sure it's from God. Over time, you'll begin to recognize patterns in how God communicates with you specifically. You'll start to distinguish between your own thoughts and the gentle promptings of the Holy Spirit. You'll develop confidence in recognizing when God is responding to your prayers and guiding your decisions.

The second crucial preparation is learning to approach scripture as a means of personal encounter rather than just information gathering. Most believers read the Bible to learn facts about God, understand biblical history, or find verses that support what they already believe. But scripture is meant to be a living conversation between you and God where He speaks to your current circumstances through His written word.

Before you read any Bible passage, ask the Holy Spirit to speak to you personally through that day's scripture. Read slowly, pausing whenever a verse or phrase stands out to you. Ask God specific questions about how that passage applies to your current situation, relationships, or spiritual growth areas. Give Him permission to challenge your thinking, correct your attitudes, or guide your decisions through His word.

After reading, spend time reflecting on what stood out to you and why. Ask God what He wants you to do with what you've just read. Look for one specific way to apply that day's scripture to your actual life circumstances. This transforms Bible reading from an intellectual exercise into a practical tool for ongoing communion with God.

The third preparation involves clearing your heart of expectations about how God should communicate with you based on other people's spiritual experiences. God speaks to different people in different ways, and He may communicate with you very differently than He communicates with your pastor, your friends, or the authors of Christian books you've read. Some people sense God's presence through emotions and feelings. Others recognize His guidance through logical thoughts and clear reasoning. Some hear His voice through other people's words while others sense His direction through circumstances and opportunities.

Pay attention to how you naturally process information and make decisions in other areas of your life because God often uses your existing personality and thinking patterns to communicate with you. If you're naturally analytical, He might guide you through logical reasoning and clear thinking. If you're naturally intuitive, He might speak through gut feelings and sudden insights. If you're naturally relational, He might use conversations with other people to confirm His direction for your life.

Don't try to force yourself to experience God the same way other believers do. Instead, ask Him to show you how He's uniquely designed you to recognize His presence and respond to His voice. Be patient with yourself as you learn to distinguish His communication from your own thoughts, emotions, and desires. This discernment develops over time through consistent practice and honest evaluation of the results.

The fourth preparation is developing realistic expectations about the process of building intimate relationship with God. Spiritual intimacy develops gradually through consistent communion rather than dramatic one-time encounters. Just like human relationships deepen through regular conversation and shared experiences over time, your relationship with God will deepen through daily interaction and ongoing responsiveness to His guidance.

Don't expect every prayer time to feel emotionally powerful or every Bible reading to provide life-changing insights. Some days your communion with God will feel rich and meaningful while other days it will feel routine or even difficult. The goal is consistency of connection rather than intensity of experience. God is building something lasting in your heart that can withstand difficult circumstances and dry seasons, not just creating temporary spiritual highs that fade when life gets challenging.

Focus on showing up consistently for your daily time with God rather than trying to generate specific feelings or experiences. Trust that He is working in your heart even when you don't sense His presence clearly. Measure your spiritual growth by your increasing ability to recognize His guidance and your growing confidence in His love rather than by the emotional intensity of your devotional times.

Chapter 1 Call to Growth

Your spiritual hunger is not a problem to solve but a gift to steward, and the way you respond to this holy dissatisfaction will determine whether you spend the rest of your life settling for surface-level Christianity or discover the intimate communion with God that your soul is craving. The choice is entirely yours, but the choice must be made intentionally through specific actions rather than good intentions or wishful thinking.

Starting tomorrow morning, commit to spending fifteen minutes in conversational prayer where you talk with God rather than just talking at God. Set a timer for seven minutes and share with Him exactly how you're feeling about your current spiritual state. Tell Him about your hunger for deeper relationship, your frustration with shallow Christianity, and your desire to know Him personally rather than just knowing about Him. Be completely honest about your spiritual disappointments and your longing for authentic encounter with His presence.

When the timer goes off, reset it for eight minutes and sit quietly to listen for His response. Don't expect to hear an audible voice, but pay attention to any thoughts, impressions, or insights that come to mind during this listening time. Write down whatever surfaces, even if you're not sure it's from God or if it seems insignificant. Over time, you'll learn to recognize how God specifically communicates with you through this practice of attentive listening.

Choose one specific religious activity or church program that leaves you feeling spiritually empty and make the decision to step away from it for the next thirty days.

This might be a Bible study that focuses on information rather than transformation, a small group that stays at surface level, or a church service that feels more like performance than worship. Use the time you would normally spend in that activity for personal communion with God instead.

During those reclaimed hours, experiment with different ways of connecting with God's presence until you discover what actually feeds your soul. Try extended times of worship music, silent meditation on scripture, journaling your prayers, taking prayer walks, or any other spiritual practice that creates space for intimate encounter with Jesus. Pay attention to which practices leave you feeling spiritually nourished rather than spiritually drained.

Identify one person in your life who might not understand your decision to prioritize personal relationship with God over religious activity and prepare yourself mentally for their potential disappointment or criticism. Practice explaining your spiritual hunger in terms they can understand without defending your choices or trying to convince them to make similar changes. Your job is to follow God's leading in your own spiritual growth, not to manage other people's reactions to your spiritual maturity.

Create a simple spiritual journal where you can track

your growing ability to recognize God's voice and sense His presence throughout each day. At the end of each day, write down one specific way you sensed God's involvement in your circumstances, noticed His guidance in a decision, or experienced His presence during your devotional time. This practice will help you recognize patterns in how God communicates with you and build your confidence in His active involvement in your daily life.

Set a specific date thirty days from today when you'll evaluate your spiritual growth and decide which practices to continue, modify, or abandon based on their actual impact on your intimacy with God rather than their reputation or popularity among other believers. Spiritual disciplines are tools for building relationship with Jesus, not ends in themselves, and you have permission to adjust your spiritual practices based on what actually deepens your communion with Him.

Finally, ask God to give you one specific person who shares your hunger for deeper spiritual intimacy so you don't have to navigate this journey completely alone. This might be someone from your current church community, a believer from another church, or someone you haven't met yet who God will bring into your life. Pray for spiritual friendship with someone who will encourage your growth rather than trying to keep you satisfied with shallow Christianity.

These steps will begin moving you from the realm of believing about God into the realm of knowing God personally. They will create the foundation for the kind of intimate relationship with Jesus that transforms everything about how you think, feel, and respond to life's challenges. They will satisfy the spiritual hunger that has been driving your holy dissatisfaction with surface-level faith.

Your spiritual hunger is God's invitation to something better than anything you've experienced before. Accept the invitation.

Chapter 2 | Learning to Hear God's Voice

The sheep that are My own hear My voice and listen to Me; I know them, and they follow Me. John 10:27 AMP

God speaks to you every single day, but most of what He says gets lost in the noise of your own thoughts, emotions, and the constant chatter of daily life. Learning to recognize His voice isn't about developing some mystical spiritual ability that only certain believers possess. It's about training your spiritual ears to distinguish His gentle communication from all the other voices competing for your attention throughout each day.

The problem isn't that God has stopped speaking or that He only talks to spiritually elite believers. The problem is that you've never been taught how to listen for His voice or how to recognize the subtle ways He responds when you pray. You've been conditioned to expect God to communicate like a human being with audible words and obvious signs, but He usually speaks through gentle impressions, quiet thoughts, and the still small voice that whispers to your spirit rather than your ears.

Your ability to hear God's voice directly impacts every area of your spiritual life and practical decision-making. When you can't distinguish His guidance from your own reasoning, you end up making choices based on limited human wisdom instead of His perfect knowledge of your circumstances. When you can't recognize His comfort during difficult seasons, you struggle with anxiety and fear instead of resting in His peace. When you can't sense His direction for your relationships, career, and daily decisions, you live with constant uncertainty about whether you're living according to His will.

Learning to hear God's voice transforms prayer from a one-sided conversation into genuine dialogue where you speak and He responds, where you ask questions and He provides answers, where you share your concerns and He offers His perspective. It changes Bible reading from information gathering into personal encounter where God speaks directly to your current circumstances through His written word. It turns your daily life into ongoing communion where you recognize His involvement, guidance, and presence as normal parts of your everyday experience.

Why You Struggle to Recognize When God Speaks

Your mind processes thousands of thoughts every day, and most of those thoughts feel like they're coming from you because you've never learned to distinguish between thoughts that originate from your own reasoning and thoughts that are actually God speaking to your spirit. When the Holy Spirit brings a scripture verse to mind during a difficult situation, you assume you just remembered something you read before. When God gives you sudden insight about how to handle a relationship conflict, you think you just figured it out on your own. When He provides peace about a decision you've been worried about, you credit your own logic rather than recognizing His guidance.

This confusion happens because God usually communicates through your existing thought patterns rather than overriding them with obviously supernatural messages. He works through your personality, your natural way of processing information, and your normal thinking processes to guide your decisions and speak to your circumstances. This means His voice often feels like your own thoughts, which makes it easy to miss or dismiss His communication as mere human reasoning.

Most believers also struggle to hear God's voice because they're listening for the wrong kind of communication. Church culture has taught you to expect God to speak through dramatic revelations, powerful emotional experiences, or obvious supernatural signs that leave no room for doubt about their divine origin. When God doesn't communicate in these dramatic ways, you assume He's not speaking at all rather than learning to recognize His more subtle forms of communication.

God rarely speaks through dramatic supernatural encounters because He wants to build ongoing relationship with you rather than just providing occasional spiritual experiences. Dramatic revelations create temporary spiritual highs, but they don't develop the intimate communion that comes from learning to recognize His voice in daily conversation. He speaks quietly and gently because He wants you to draw close enough to hear Him, to pay attention to His communication, and to develop the spiritual sensitivity that comes from regular dialogue with His presence.

Your emotional state also significantly impacts your ability to recognize God's voice. When you're anxious, stressed, or emotionally overwhelmed, your mind becomes so busy processing your feelings that you can't distinguish

God's gentle communication from your own worried thoughts. When you're angry or frustrated, your emotions create so much internal noise that His still small voice gets drowned out by your own reactions. When you're depressed or discouraged, you filter everything through negative thinking patterns that make it difficult to recognize His encouragement or guidance.

This is why consistent spiritual disciplines like daily prayer and scripture reading are so important for developing your ability to hear God's voice. These practices create regular opportunities for you to commune with God when your emotions are calm and your mind is focused, which helps you learn to recognize how He specifically communicates with you. As you become familiar with His voice during peaceful times, you'll gradually learn to recognize His communication even during stressful or emotionally difficult seasons.

Many believers also struggle to hear God's voice because they're unconsciously afraid of what He might say to them. They worry that He'll ask them to do something difficult, give up something they enjoy, or make changes they don't want to make. This fear creates internal resistance that blocks their ability to receive His communication clearly. They ask for His guidance while simultaneously hoping He won't give them specific direction that might require obedience or sacrifice.

God knows when you're not really ready to hear His voice, and He often waits to speak clearly until you've genuinely surrendered your will to His and become willing to follow His guidance regardless of what it might cost you. This doesn't mean He's withholding communication to punish you, but rather that He's waiting for you to reach a place of genuine openness where you can receive His direction without internal resistance or rebellion.

Your expectations about how God should communicate also create barriers to recognizing His actual voice. If you're expecting Him to speak through dramatic emotional experiences but He's actually trying to guide you through quiet logical reasoning, you'll miss His communication entirely. If you're waiting for Him to speak through other people but He's trying to communicate directly to your spirit through scripture meditation, you'll keep looking for His voice in the wrong places.

God speaks to different people in different ways based on how He's uniquely designed their personalities and thinking patterns. Some people recognize His voice through sudden insights and intuitive understanding. Others sense His guidance through logical analysis and clear reasoning.

Some hear Him through scripture verses that suddenly become personally relevant, while others recognize His direction through circumstances and open doors. Your job is to discover how He specifically communicates with you rather than trying to force Him to speak the way He speaks to other believers.

Finally, many believers struggle to hear God's voice because they don't create adequate space in their lives for His communication. They pray while driving to work, read scripture while eating breakfast, and try to commune with God while multitasking through busy schedules. But recognizing God's voice requires focused attention, quiet space, and unhurried time where you can listen for His response to your prayers.

When your life is constantly busy and your mind is always occupied with tasks, responsibilities, and distractions, you don't have the mental or emotional capacity to recognize God's subtle communication. His voice gets lost in the noise of your overscheduled life. Learning to hear God requires intentionally creating space for His communication and protecting that space from the constant demands of daily life.

How God Actually Communicates with You

God's primary method of communication is through

His written word, but not in the way most believers have been taught to expect. He doesn't just speak through random Bible verses that catch your attention or through daily devotional readings that provide general encouragement. He speaks through specific passages that directly address your current circumstances, relationships, and decisions when you learn how to read scripture as ongoing conversation with His presence rather than just information about His character.

When you approach Bible reading with specific questions about your life and ask the Holy Spirit to speak to you personally through His word, He will guide you to passages that provide exactly the wisdom, comfort, or direction you need for your current situation. This might happen through your regular scripture reading plan, through verses that suddenly come to mind during the day, or through passages that other believers share with you at exactly the right moment. The key is learning to recognize when God is using His written word to speak directly to your circumstances.

This kind of personal communication through scripture requires you to move beyond reading Bible verses for general spiritual inspiration and start reading them as God's specific response to your prayers and questions.

Before you open your Bible each day, tell God exactly what you're dealing with and ask Him to speak to you about those specific issues through His word. Then read with expectant attention, looking for connections between the passage and your actual life circumstances.

God also speaks through what many believers call the still small voice, which is actually the Holy Spirit communicating directly to your spirit through thoughts, impressions, and gentle inner knowing that feels different from your normal thinking patterns. This communication usually comes as sudden insights about how to handle difficult situations, clear understanding about decisions you need to make, or peaceful confidence about directions you should take.

The still small voice often manifests as thoughts that seem to come from nowhere, ideas that you know you didn't generate through your own reasoning, or solutions to problems that suddenly become obvious even though you've been struggling with them for weeks or months. These thoughts typically align perfectly with biblical principles, bring peace rather than anxiety, and provide practical wisdom for your specific circumstances.

Learning to recognize the still small voice requires paying attention to the difference between thoughts that feel like your normal mental processing and thoughts that seem to drop into your mind from an outside source. God's thoughts usually bring clarity where there was confusion, peace where there was anxiety, and wisdom that goes beyond your natural understanding of the situation. They often provide perspective that you wouldn't have considered on your own and solutions that address the root of problems rather than just surface symptoms.

God frequently communicates through circumstances and opportunities that align with His will for your life, but this form of guidance requires spiritual discernment to distinguish between doors that God is opening and opportunities that simply appeal to your natural desires or ambitions. Divine opportunities typically come with internal peace, align with biblical principles, and contribute to your spiritual growth and God's purposes rather than just your personal comfort or success.

When God is guiding you through circumstances, you'll often notice that multiple factors line up in ways that seem too coordinated to be coincidental. The right people appear at the right time with the right information or opportunities. Resources become available just when you need them. Obstacles that seemed impossible to overcome suddenly resolve themselves. Doors open that you couldn't have opened through your own efforts.

But not every open door is from God, and not every closed door means He's saying no to your request. Sometimes God closes doors to protect you from situations that would harm your spiritual growth or derail His plans for your life. Sometimes He opens doors as tests to see if you'll choose His will over your own desires. Learning to discern which circumstances represent His guidance requires combining attention to external opportunities with internal peace and confirmation through scripture and prayer.

God also speaks through other believers, but this communication typically comes through casual conversations rather than formal spiritual counsel. He might use a comment from a coworker to give you insight about a relationship problem, a question from a friend to help you recognize an attitude that needs to change, or encouragement from a fellow believer to confirm a direction He's already been leading you to consider.

When God speaks through other people, they usually don't realize they're delivering a message from Him to you. The conversation feels natural and unforced, but their words address exactly what you've been praying about or struggling with. Their perspective provides clarity about situations you've been confused about, or their questions help you recognize truth you've been avoiding.

This form of divine communication requires wisdom to distinguish between human opinions that happen to align with your preferences and actual messages from God that address your spiritual needs. God's communication through other people typically challenges you to grow spiritually, aligns with biblical truth, and brings peace rather than confusion about His will for your circumstances.

God sometimes communicates through dreams and visions, but this form of guidance is less common than most believers expect and requires careful interpretation to distinguish between divine communication and normal psychological processing of daily experiences. Biblical dreams and visions typically provide clear direction about specific situations, align perfectly with scripture, and come with internal confirmation that they represent actual communication from God rather than subconscious wish fulfillment.

When God does speak through dreams or visions, the message usually addresses significant decisions or spiritual growth areas rather than minor daily concerns. The communication provides wisdom that goes beyond your natural understanding and often includes symbolic elements that become clear as you pray for interpretation and seek confirmation through scripture and circumstances.

Most importantly, God communicates through the internal peace or unrest that you feel about different decisions and directions. When you're considering choices that align with His will, you'll typically experience deep peace even if the decision involves difficulty or sacrifice. When you're considering choices that don't align with His purposes, you'll often feel internal unrest, anxiety, or confusion even if the option seems attractive from a human perspective.

This internal guidance system requires you to pay attention to your spiritual responses rather than just your emotional reactions to different possibilities. Spiritual peace comes from your spirit recognizing alignment with God's will, while emotional excitement might simply reflect your natural preferences or desires. Learning to distinguish between spiritual and emotional responses takes practice, but it becomes one of the most reliable ways to recognize God's guidance in daily decision-making.

Creating Space for God to Respond

Most believers never hear God's voice clearly because they never create adequate space for His response to their prayers, treating prayer like a spiritual monologue where they talk at God rather than a genuine conversation where they speak and then listen for His reply. Learning to hear God requires intentionally building listening time into every prayer session and protecting that time from the mental distractions that prevent you from recognizing His communication.

Start every prayer time by acknowledging that you expect God to respond to what you're about to share with Him and that you're prepared to listen for His reply. This simple shift in expectation changes prayer from religious duty into genuine dialogue. Tell God that you want to hear His perspective on your circumstances, His guidance for your decisions, and His comfort for your concerns. Let Him know that you're not just presenting requests but seeking conversation with His presence.

After you finish sharing your prayers, set a timer for at least five minutes and sit in complete silence with your attention focused on listening for God's response. Don't fill this time with more talking, additional requests, or mental planning for the rest of your day. Simply sit quietly with an attitude of expectant listening, paying attention to any thoughts, impressions, or insights that come to mind during this focused waiting period.

During your listening time, write down whatever

comes to mind even if you're not sure it's from God or if it seems unimportant. Don't edit or evaluate what you're receiving during the listening period itself. Simply record thoughts, impressions, scripture verses, or insights that surface while you're waiting for God's response. You can evaluate the significance and source of what you received after your prayer time is complete.

Many believers struggle with listening prayer because their minds immediately fill with distracting thoughts about work responsibilities, family concerns, or daily tasks as soon as they try to sit quietly. This mental noise is normal and doesn't mean you're doing something wrong or that God isn't trying to communicate with you. Learning to listen for God's voice requires developing the ability to distinguish between random mental chatter and actual communication from His spirit.

When distracting thoughts arise during your listening time, acknowledge them briefly and then redirect your attention to listening for God's voice. Don't fight against the distractions or feel guilty about having a busy mind. Simply notice when your thoughts have wandered and gently refocus on expectant listening. This skill improves with practice, and your ability to maintain focused attention during prayer will increase over time.

Create a consistent physical environment for your listening prayer that minimizes external distractions and helps your mind associate that space with communion with God. This might be a specific chair in your bedroom, a corner of your living room, or an outdoor location where you can sit quietly without interruption. Having a designated prayer space helps train your mind to shift into listening mode more quickly and creates environmental cues that support focused attention on God's presence.

Turn off all electronic devices during your prayer and listening time to eliminate the constant mental interruption of notifications, messages, and digital distractions. Your phone, computer, and other devices create subtle anxiety even when they're not actively demanding your attention because your mind remains partially focused on potential incoming communication. Complete disconnection from digital devices is essential for developing the mental stillness that allows you to recognize God's voice.

Establish a consistent daily time for listening prayer when your mind is naturally calm and your schedule is least likely to be interrupted by urgent responsibilities. For most people, early morning provides the best opportunity for focused communion with God because your mind hasn't yet become occupied with the day's tasks and concerns.

Evening can also work well if you can create genuine quiet time after completing your daily responsibilities.

The key is consistency rather than duration. Fifteen minutes of focused listening prayer every day will develop your ability to hear God's voice much more effectively than occasional longer prayer sessions when you remember or feel motivated. God wants to build ongoing dialogue with you rather than just providing occasional spiritual experiences, and consistent daily communion creates the relationship foundation that allows His voice to become familiar and recognizable.

Practice asking God specific questions during your prayer time and then listening for His specific answers rather than just sharing general concerns and hoping for vague encouragement. Instead of praying "God, please help me with my job situation," ask "God, what specific steps should I take to address the conflict with my supervisor?" Instead of "Please bless my family," ask "How can I better serve my spouse's emotional needs this week?"

Specific questions invite specific answers, and God delights in providing practical wisdom for your actual circumstances when you ask for His guidance in concrete terms. General prayers often receive general responses that are difficult to recognize as divine communication, while specific questions create opportunities for clear, practical guidance that you can immediately apply to your daily life.

Keep a prayer journal where you record both your questions to God and the responses you receive during your listening times. This practice serves multiple purposes: it helps you remember what you sensed during prayer, it allows you to track patterns in how God communicates with you, and it provides a record of His faithfulness that you can review during seasons when His voice seems less clear.

Review your prayer journal regularly to look for themes in God's communication and to evaluate the accuracy of what you thought you heard from Him. Over time, you'll begin to recognize the difference between your own thoughts and God's actual responses. You'll notice that His communication typically brings peace, aligns with biblical principles, and provides wisdom that goes beyond your natural understanding of situations.

Don't expect every listening session to produce obvious communication from God or feel frustrated when some prayer times feel quiet or unproductive. God is always present and always listening, but He doesn't always respond immediately to every question or concern. Sometimes He's waiting for you to take action on guidance

He's already given before providing additional direction. Sometimes He's using quiet seasons to develop your faith and dependence on His character rather than His communication.

The goal of listening prayer is building ongoing relationship with God rather than just receiving answers to your questions. Even when you don't sense clear communication during your listening time, you're still developing spiritual intimacy through the practice of expectant waiting in His presence. This intimacy becomes the foundation for recognizing His voice more clearly during future prayer sessions and throughout your daily life.

Testing What You Think You Hear

Not every thought that comes to mind during prayer originates from God, and learning to distinguish between divine communication, your own reasoning, and spiritual deception is one of the most critical skills for mature believers who want to follow God's guidance confidently. The enemy of your soul is perfectly capable of providing religious-sounding thoughts that lead you away from God's actual will, and your own desires can masquerade as spiritual guidance when you want something badly enough.

The first test for any spiritual impression is alignment

with scripture, because God will never communicate anything that contradicts His written word or violates the principles He's established in the Bible. If the guidance you think you're receiving encourages you to act in ways that conflict with biblical commands, compromise your integrity, or harm other people, you can be certain it's not coming from God regardless of how spiritual or compelling it might feel.

This doesn't mean God's guidance will always be easy or comfortable, because He often calls believers to difficult obedience that requires sacrifice and spiritual growth. But His guidance will always align with His character as revealed in scripture and will never encourage you to sin, deceive others, or act in ways that damage your relationship with Him or harm the people He's called you to love.

Apply the biblical test by asking specific questions about any guidance you think you've received: Does this align with what scripture teaches about God's character and His will for believers? Does this guidance encourage me to grow in love, faith, and obedience, or does it appeal to my selfishness, pride, or desire for comfort? Would following this direction bring glory to God and benefit to others, or would it primarily serve my own interests and preferences?

The second test is internal peace, because authentic

guidance from God typically brings deep spiritual peace even when it involves difficulty or sacrifice. When God is directing your steps, you'll experience what the Bible calls "peace that passes understanding" about the direction He's leading you to take. This peace might coexist with natural anxiety about challenging circumstances, but underneath the surface emotions, you'll sense spiritual confidence that you're following His will.

Guidance that doesn't come from God typically produces internal unrest, anxiety, or confusion even when the suggested course of action seems attractive from a human perspective. Your spirit recognizes when direction doesn't align with God's will and responds with unease that persists despite your mental attempts to convince yourself that the guidance makes sense.

Pay attention to your spiritual response rather than just your emotional reaction when evaluating potential guidance. Emotional excitement about an opportunity doesn't necessarily indicate divine direction, and emotional reluctance about a difficult path doesn't necessarily mean God isn't calling you in that direction. Spiritual peace or unrest provides more reliable confirmation about God's will than your natural emotional preferences.

The third test is practical wisdom, because God's

guidance typically demonstrates supernatural wisdom that addresses the root issues in your circumstances rather than just providing temporary solutions that appeal to your immediate desires. Divine direction often includes perspective that you wouldn't have considered on your own and solutions that take into account factors you hadn't fully recognized.

Guidance from God usually addresses not just your immediate concerns but also your long-term spiritual growth and His larger purposes for your life. It provides direction that serves His kingdom rather than just your personal comfort, and it often includes elements that will develop your character and deepen your dependence on His strength rather than your own abilities.

Evaluate potential guidance by asking: Does this direction demonstrate wisdom that goes beyond my natural understanding? Does it address the real issues in my situation rather than just surface problems? Will following this guidance contribute to my spiritual maturity and God's purposes, or does it primarily serve my immediate wants and preferences?

The fourth test is confirmation through circumstances, because God typically confirms His guidance through external validation when He's directing you to make significant decisions or changes. This confirmation might come through other believers who provide similar counsel without knowing what you've been praying about, through opportunities that align with the direction you sense Him leading, or through resources that become available to support the path He's calling you to take.

However, be careful not to force circumstances to fit the guidance you want to receive or to interpret every positive development as confirmation of your preferred direction. True confirmation comes naturally without manipulation and typically includes multiple factors that align in ways that seem too coordinated to be coincidental.

Ask God to provide clear confirmation for any major guidance you think you've received and be willing to wait for that confirmation before taking action. God is not in a hurry, and He's perfectly capable of providing obvious validation when He wants you to move forward with confidence. If you have to strain to find confirmation or convince yourself that unclear circumstances represent divine validation, you probably need to wait for clearer direction.

The fifth test is the fruit that results from following the guidance, because authentic direction from God produces spiritual fruit in your life and positive impact on the people around you. When you follow God's actual guidance, you'll experience increased peace, spiritual growth, and deeper intimacy with His presence. Your obedience to His direction will typically benefit other people and advance His purposes rather than just serving your personal interests.

Guidance that doesn't come from God often produces anxiety, spiritual confusion, or negative consequences that harm your relationships and hinder your spiritual growth. Even when following false guidance initially seems successful from a worldly perspective, it ultimately leads to spiritual emptiness and distance from God's presence.

Evaluate the results of following guidance you thought came from God by asking: Has following this direction increased my peace and spiritual intimacy with God, or has it created anxiety and spiritual confusion? Has my obedience to this guidance benefited other people and advanced God's purposes, or has it primarily served my own interests? Am I experiencing spiritual growth and increased dependence on God, or am I becoming more self-reliant and distant from His presence?

Finally, seek counsel from mature believers who know you well and have demonstrated wisdom in their own spiritual lives, but be careful to distinguish between human advice and spiritual confirmation. Other believers can provide valuable perspective about your circumstances and help you evaluate potential guidance, but their opinions don't automatically represent God's will for your life.

When seeking counsel about guidance you think you've received, share the situation honestly without revealing what you think God has already told you. Ask for their prayers and perspective, then evaluate whether their counsel aligns with the direction you sensed during your own prayer time. God often uses other believers to confirm His guidance, but He can also speak to you directly even when other people don't understand or agree with the direction He's leading you to take.

Chapter 2 Call to Growth

Your ability to recognize God's voice will determine whether you spend the rest of your life making decisions based on limited human wisdom or learning to follow His perfect guidance for every area of your circumstances, relationships, and spiritual growth. This skill develops through consistent practice rather than spiritual talent, and the specific steps you take this week will establish patterns that either increase or decrease your sensitivity to His communication.

Tomorrow morning, begin each day with ten minutes of focused listening prayer using this specific format: spend three minutes sharing your concerns and questions with God, then set a timer for seven minutes and sit in complete silence with your attention focused entirely on listening for His response. Write down every thought, impression, or insight that comes to mind during those seven minutes regardless of whether you think it's from God or how significant it seems.

After one week of daily listening prayer, review everything you wrote down during your silent times and look for patterns in the type of thoughts and impressions you received. Circle anything that provided practical wisdom for your circumstances, brought you peace about difficult situations, or gave you insight that went beyond your normal understanding. These patterns will help you begin recognizing how God specifically communicates with you.

Choose one specific decision you need to make in the next thirty days and commit to seeking God's guidance for that decision through daily prayer rather than just relying on your own reasoning or other people's advice. Each day, ask God the same specific question about this decision, then listen carefully for His response. Keep a record of any guidance you receive and look for confirmation through scripture, circumstances, and internal peace.

Identify the time of day when your mind is naturally most calm and focused, then establish that as your consistent daily appointment for listening prayer. Protect this time from interruptions by turning off all electronic devices, finding a quiet location, and informing family members or roommates that you're not available during this period. Consistency of timing helps train your mind to shift into listening mode more quickly.

Select three specific Bible passages that address current challenges in your life and commit to meditating on one passage each day for the next week, asking God to speak to you personally through His written word about your actual circumstances. Before reading each passage, tell God exactly what you're dealing with and ask Him to give you His perspective through that day's scripture. Write down any connections you notice between the biblical text and your current situation.

Practice distinguishing between your own thoughts and potential communication from God by paying attention to thoughts that seem to come from outside your normal reasoning process. When you experience sudden insights about how to handle difficult situations, unexpected solutions to problems you've been struggling with, or clear understanding about decisions you need to make, write down these experiences and evaluate them using the biblical tests for spiritual guidance.

Find one mature believer who demonstrates wisdom in their spiritual life and ask them to pray with you about learning to recognize God's voice more clearly. Share your desire to develop better listening skills in prayer and ask for their accountability in maintaining consistent daily communion with God. Don't ask them to interpret what you think God is saying to you, but do ask them to pray for your spiritual discernment and growth in intimacy with Jesus.

Finally, commit to testing any significant guidance you think you receive from God by waiting for confirmation through multiple sources before taking major action. Establish the practice of seeking confirmation through scripture, internal peace, practical wisdom, and circumstances before making important decisions based on what you believe God has told you. This patience protects you from acting on false guidance while building your confidence in recognizing His authentic voice.

These practices will systematically develop your ability to recognize when God is speaking to you and distinguish His voice from your own thoughts, emotions, and desires. They will transform your prayer life from religious monologue into genuine dialogue and establish the foundation for living with confident awareness of God's daily guidance in every area of your life.

God is speaking to you every day. These steps will teach you how to listen.

Chapter 3 | Scripture as Personal Encounter

Come close to God [with a contrite heart] and He will come close to you. Wash your hands, you sinners; and purify your hearts, you double-minded [people].
James 4:8 AMP

You've been reading the Bible like a textbook when God intended it to be a love letter, studying His word for information about His character when He designed it to be ongoing conversation with His presence in your daily circumstances. This fundamental misunderstanding of scripture's purpose explains why you can read Bible verses every day for years while still feeling spiritually empty and disconnected from the God who wrote them specifically to communicate with you personally.

The Bible isn't just a collection of ancient stories, moral principles, and theological concepts that provide general guidance for Christian living. Every passage contains God's active voice speaking directly to your current relationships, decisions, and spiritual growth areas when you learn how to read His word as personal encounter rather than historical information. The same Holy Spirit who inspired the original authors to write these words is present with you today, ready to apply their meaning to your specific circumstances in ways that provide exactly the wisdom, comfort, and direction you need.

When you approach scripture as personal conversation with God rather than academic study material, Bible reading transforms from religious duty into intimate dialogue where He responds to your prayers, addresses your concerns, and guides your decisions through His written word. You begin to experience what believers throughout history have discovered: God's word is alive and active, sharper than any sword, and capable of speaking directly to the deepest needs of your heart when you create space for personal encounter with His presence through focused scripture meditation.

This shift from information gathering to personal encounter requires learning specific techniques for allowing the Holy Spirit to speak to you through biblical text, but most believers have never been taught these skills because church culture emphasizes knowing about God's word rather than communing with God through His word. You've learned how to analyze scripture, memorize verses, and discuss biblical principles, but you haven't learned how to position your heart to receive personal communication from God's spirit through the passages you read each day.

Moving Beyond Bible Study to Bible Communion

Traditional Bible study focuses on understanding what scripture meant to its original audience, analyzing historical context, and extracting universal principles that apply to all believers in all circumstances. This approach treats the Bible like any other ancient text that requires scholarly interpretation to unlock its meaning, but it misses the supernatural dimension that makes God's word fundamentally different from human literature. Scripture is not just inspired writing about God; it's God's active voice speaking to you personally through the ministry of the Holy Spirit who lives in your heart.

Bible communion begins with the recognition that the same Spirit who inspired the biblical authors to write these words is present with you now, ready to apply their meaning to your specific circumstances in ways that provide exactly what you need for your current spiritual growth and practical decision-making. This means every passage contains both its historical meaning and its personal application to your life today, and the Holy Spirit delights in revealing both dimensions when you approach scripture with expectant faith rather than just intellectual curiosity.

The difference between Bible study and Bible communion is the difference between reading someone else's mail and receiving your own personal correspondence from God. Bible study asks "What did this passage mean to its original readers?" while Bible communion asks "What is God saying to me personally through this passage today?" Bible study seeks to understand biblical principles, while Bible communion seeks to encounter God's presence and receive His specific guidance for your actual life circumstances.

This doesn't mean historical context and accurate interpretation are unimportant, because God's personal communication through scripture always aligns with the text's original meaning and never contradicts sound biblical interpretation. But it does mean that understanding the historical meaning is only the beginning of what God wants to accomplish through His word in your daily life. He wants to move beyond teaching you about His character and His ways to actually communicating with you about your specific relationships, decisions, and spiritual growth areas through the passages you read.

Bible communion requires approaching scripture with specific questions about your current circumstances and asking the Holy Spirit to speak to you about those situations through His written word. Instead of reading to learn general biblical principles, you read to receive God's specific perspective on the challenges you're facing, the decisions you need to make, and the spiritual growth areas where you need His guidance and encouragement.

Before opening your Bible each day, spend a few minutes telling God exactly what you're dealing with in your relationships, work, family, spiritual life, and decision-making. Share your concerns, questions, fears, and hopes with Him, then ask Him to speak to you about these specific issues through that day's scripture reading. This creates the context for personal encounter and positions your heart to recognize when He's addressing your actual circumstances through biblical text.

Read with expectant attention, looking for connections between the passage and your current situation rather than just trying to understand what the text teaches in general terms. Pay attention to verses that seem to jump out at you, phrases that feel particularly relevant to your circumstances, and insights that provide new perspective on situations you've been praying about. The Holy Spirit often highlights specific portions of scripture that contain His personal response to your prayers and concerns.

When a verse or passage feels particularly relevant to your current circumstances, stop reading and spend time meditating on that specific text. Ask God why that particular verse caught your attention and how it applies to your situation. Ask Him to show you what He wants you to understand, feel, or do in response to what you've just read. This focused meditation creates space for the Holy Spirit to provide specific application and personal guidance through His written word.

Bible communion also requires reading scripture slowly enough to actually hear God's voice through the text rather than just processing information quickly. Most believers read the Bible too fast to recognize when God is speaking to them personally through specific passages. They're focused on covering a certain amount of material or completing their reading plan rather than creating space for encounter with God's presence through His word.

Slow down your reading pace and give the Holy Spirit time to speak to you through each passage. Read each verse at least twice, pausing between readings to consider what God might be saying to you through that particular text. Look for words or phrases that seem especially significant, verses that bring you comfort or challenge, and passages that provide new insight into situations you've been praying about.

Don't worry about covering large amounts of scripture in each reading session. It's better to encounter God personally through one verse that speaks directly to your heart than to read entire chapters without experiencing His presence or receiving His guidance. The goal is communion with God through His word, not completion of religious assignments or accumulation of biblical knowledge.

Keep a journal specifically for recording what you sense God saying to you through scripture each day. Write down verses that feel particularly relevant to your circumstances, insights that provide new perspective on your situations, and specific ways you sense Him guiding you through His written word. This practice helps you remember what you've received during your Bible reading and creates a record of God's personal communication with you through scripture over time.

Review your scripture journal regularly to look for patterns in how God speaks to you through His word and to see how His guidance through biblical text has proven faithful in your actual life circumstances. This review builds your confidence in recognizing His voice through scripture and helps you become more sensitive to His personal communication through future Bible reading sessions.

Finally, respond to what you receive during Bible communion by taking specific action based on God's guidance rather than just appreciating the insights He provides. When He shows you areas where you need to grow spiritually, take concrete steps toward that growth. When He provides comfort for difficult circumstances, rest in that comfort and share it with others who need encouragement. When He gives you direction for decisions, follow that direction with confidence and obedience.

Bible communion becomes increasingly meaningful as you demonstrate faithfulness in responding to what God shows you through His word. He delights in providing more specific guidance and deeper insights to believers who consistently act on what they receive during their scripture reading times.

Letting the Bible Speak to Your Heart

The Amplified Bible reveals layers of meaning in God's word that remain hidden in traditional translations, providing access to the rich depth of the original Hebrew and Greek texts that can transform your understanding of familiar passages and open new dimensions of personal encounter with God's voice through scripture. This translation doesn't just give you the basic meaning of biblical text; it shows you the full range of what God was communicating through the original languages, allowing you to experience the complete richness of His message rather than just surface-level understanding.

When you read that God loves you in a traditional translation, the Amplified Bible shows you that He loves you unconditionally, unalterably, and sacrificially, with a love that is steadfast, loyal, and completely devoted to your highest good regardless of your performance or circumstances. This expanded understanding transforms a general statement about God's love into a specific revelation of how He actually feels about you personally, providing the kind of detailed insight that builds unshakeable confidence in His heart toward you.

The Amplified Bible's expanded translations help you recognize when God is speaking to your specific circumstances through scripture because they provide more complete context for understanding how biblical principles apply to your actual life situations. Instead of reading that you should trust God, you discover that you should trust Him completely, confidently, and without reservation, leaning on Him with full confidence in His wisdom, power, and goodness. This specificity helps you understand exactly what trusting God looks like in practical terms and gives you clear direction for how to respond to His guidance.

Use the Amplified Bible's expanded translations as starting points for deeper meditation on passages that feel relevant to your current circumstances. When you encounter a verse that seems to address your situation, read it several times slowly, paying attention to each amplified word and phrase. Ask the Holy Spirit to show you why He's highlighting that particular passage and how the expanded meaning applies to your specific challenges, decisions, or spiritual growth areas.

The additional words and phrases in the Amplified Bible often provide exactly the encouragement, correction, or guidance you need for your current situation. A passage about God's faithfulness might include amplifications that address your specific fears about the future. A verse about prayer might contain expanded language that answers questions you've been asking about how to commune with God more effectively. A passage about relationships might include details that provide wisdom for specific conflicts or challenges you're facing with family members, friends, or coworkers.

Pay special attention to the amplified words that describe God's character, His promises, and His heart toward His people, because these expanded descriptions often provide personal encouragement that addresses your deepest spiritual needs and insecurities. When you read that God is your refuge, the Amplified Bible shows you that He is your shelter, your place of safety, your stronghold, and your high tower where you can find complete protection from every threat and challenge.

This kind of detailed description helps you understand not just that God cares about your circumstances but exactly how He wants to be involved in protecting, providing, and guiding you through every difficulty you face. The amplified language transforms abstract theological concepts into concrete realities that you can apply immediately to your current challenges and concerns.

When reading the Amplified Bible for personal encounter, focus on passages that contain promises, commands, or descriptions of God's character rather than just historical narratives or genealogical records. While every part of scripture is valuable, some passages lend themselves more readily to personal application and communion with God's presence. The Psalms, Proverbs, and New Testament letters contain particularly rich material for personal encounter because they address universal human experiences and spiritual needs.

Create a personal collection of bible passages that speak directly to your most common spiritual challenges and life circumstances. Copy these verses into a notebook or digital file where you can review them regularly, especially during seasons when you need specific encouragement, guidance, or reminders of God's faithfulness. Having easy access to passages that have previously provided personal encounter with God's presence helps you maintain spiritual strength during busy or difficult periods.

Use the Amplified Bible's expanded language to develop more specific and meaningful prayers based on what you're reading in scripture. Instead of praying general requests for God's blessing, use the amplified descriptions of His character and promises to pray specifically for the kinds of help, guidance, and provision that align with what He's revealed about Himself in His word. This creates more focused prayers that align with God's will and often receive clearer answers.

When you read that God gives wisdom generously to those who ask, the Amplified Bible shows you that He gives wisdom liberally, abundantly, and without reproach, providing exactly the insight and understanding you need for every decision and challenge. This expanded understanding helps you pray more specifically for the kind of wisdom you need and builds your confidence that God will provide detailed guidance rather than just general encouragement.

The Amplified Bible also helps you recognize when God is correcting attitudes or behaviors that need to change in your life because the expanded translations make the practical applications of biblical commands more specific and harder to ignore or rationalize. When scripture tells you to be patient, the amplified version shows you that patience includes being steadfast, persevering, and maintaining a calm spirit even when circumstances are frustrating or people are difficult.

This specificity helps you identify exact areas where you need to grow spiritually and provides clear targets for your efforts to become more like Jesus. Instead of wondering what spiritual maturity looks like in practical terms, the Amplified Bible gives you detailed descriptions of godly character qualities and behaviors that you can immediately begin developing through God's strength and grace.

Don't try to read large portions of the Amplified Bible

in single sessions because the expanded language requires more time to process and meditate on than traditional translations. Focus on smaller passages that you can read slowly and thoughtfully, giving the Holy Spirit time to highlight specific words and phrases that contain His personal communication to you. Quality of encounter is more important than quantity of material covered.

Finally, remember that the Amplified Bible is a tool for encountering God through His word, not an end in itself. The goal is not to appreciate the expanded translations but to recognize God's voice speaking to you personally through the fuller meaning of biblical text. Use the amplified language as a doorway into deeper communion with God's presence rather than just as interesting information about what scripture means in its original languages.

When Scripture Comes Alive

There comes a moment in every believer's relationship with God when scripture stops being ancient text and becomes living conversation, when Bible verses transform from inspiring quotes into personal messages that address your specific circumstances with supernatural timing and perfect relevance. This experience of scripture coming alive happens when the Holy Spirit takes biblical text and applies it directly to your current situation in ways that provide exactly the wisdom, comfort, or guidance you need at precisely the moment you need it most.

When scripture comes alive, you'll read a passage you've encountered dozens of times before and suddenly see connections to your current circumstances that were never obvious during previous readings. A verse about God's faithfulness will speak directly to your current fears about the future. A passage about forgiveness will provide specific guidance for a relationship conflict you've been struggling to resolve. A promise about God's provision will address financial concerns you've been praying about for weeks.

This supernatural application of God's word to your personal circumstances is one of the primary ways the Holy Spirit communicates with believers, but it requires creating the right conditions for encounter rather than just hoping it will happen randomly during your regular Bible reading. Scripture comes alive most often when you approach God's word with specific questions about your life and ask the Holy Spirit to speak to you about those situations through biblical text.

The key to experiencing scripture as living conversation is bringing your actual life circumstances into your Bible reading rather than trying to keep your devotional time separate from your practical concerns. God wants to speak to you about your relationships, your work, your financial decisions, your parenting challenges, your health concerns, and every other area where you need His wisdom and guidance. He's not interested in providing general spiritual inspiration that doesn't connect to your real life.

Before reading scripture each day, spend time telling God exactly what you're dealing with and asking Him to speak to you about those specific issues through His written word. Be honest about your fears, frustrations, hopes, and questions rather than trying to sound spiritual or hide your real concerns. God already knows what you're thinking and feeling, and He wants to address your actual needs rather than the needs you think you should have as a mature believer.

When you read with this kind of openness and expectation, you'll begin to notice that certain verses seem to jump off the page with relevance to your current situation. Pay attention to passages that feel particularly meaningful, verses that bring you comfort or challenge, and insights that provide new perspective on situations you've been praying about. These moments of recognition are the

Holy Spirit highlighting specific portions of scripture that contain His response to your prayers and concerns.

Scripture comes alive most powerfully during seasons of difficulty, transition, or important decision-making because these circumstances create the spiritual hunger and attention that allow you to recognize God's voice more clearly through His written word. When you're facing challenges that exceed your natural wisdom or resources, you become more sensitive to supernatural guidance and more likely to notice when God is speaking directly to your situation through biblical text.

Don't be surprised if the same passages that provided comfort or guidance during previous difficult seasons speak to you again during new challenges, because God often uses familiar scripture to provide fresh insight and encouragement for different circumstances. The Holy Spirit can apply the same biblical text to multiple situations in your life, each time revealing new dimensions of meaning that address your current needs while building on previous encounters with that passage.

When scripture comes alive with personal relevance, take time to meditate deeply on that passage rather than continuing to read additional material. Ask God why that particular verse caught your attention and how it applies specifically to your current circumstances. Ask Him what He wants you to understand, feel, or do in response to what you've just read. This focused meditation allows the Holy Spirit to provide detailed application and specific guidance through His written word.

Write down these moments when scripture speaks directly to your circumstances, including both the biblical text and your understanding of how it applies to your current situation. This creates a personal record of God's communication with you through His word that you can review during future seasons when His voice seems less clear or when you need reminders of His faithfulness in previous circumstances.

Scripture often comes alive through what seems like coincidence but is actually God's perfect timing in providing exactly the right passage at exactly the right moment. You might randomly turn to a Bible passage that addresses the exact issue you've been praying about, or someone might share a verse with you that provides specific guidance for a decision you need to make. These apparent coincidences are actually the Holy Spirit orchestrating encounters with His word that provide supernatural wisdom for your circumstances.

Pay attention to scripture that comes to your attention

through multiple sources within a short period of time, because God often confirms His communication by bringing the same passage or theme to your attention through different channels. You might read a verse during your personal devotions, hear the same passage referenced in a sermon, and have a friend mention the same biblical principle in conversation all within the same week. This kind of repetition usually indicates that God is emphasizing something important for your current spiritual growth or circumstances.

When scripture comes alive with personal application, act on what you receive rather than just appreciating the insight or feeling encouraged by the experience. If God shows you areas where you need to grow spiritually, take concrete steps toward that growth. If He provides comfort for difficult circumstances, rest in that comfort and share it with others who need encouragement. If He gives you direction for decisions, follow that direction with confidence and obedience.

Your responsiveness to God's communication through scripture directly impacts how frequently you experience these moments of living encounter with His word. The Holy Spirit provides more specific guidance and deeper insights to believers who consistently act on what they receive during their Bible reading times. Obedience to previous guidance creates the spiritual foundation for receiving clearer communication in the future.

Finally, remember that scripture coming alive is not about finding hidden meanings in biblical text or forcing passages to say what you want to hear. The Holy Spirit's application of God's word to your circumstances always aligns with sound biblical interpretation and never contradicts the clear teaching of scripture. When God speaks to you through His written word, He's providing personal application of biblical truth rather than revealing new information that isn't already contained in the text.

Trust the Holy Spirit to make scripture come alive in your personal reading times but also test what you think you're hearing against the overall teaching of God's word and seek confirmation through prayer, circumstances, and counsel from mature believers when you're making important decisions based on biblical guidance.

Chapter 3 Call to Growth

Your relationship with God's word will determine whether you spend the rest of your life knowing about His character and His ways or experiencing His personal communication through scripture that provides specific guidance for every area of your daily circumstances, relationships, and spiritual growth. The specific practices you implement this week will establish patterns that either increase or decrease your sensitivity to His voice through biblical text.

Starting tomorrow, begin each scripture reading session by spending five minutes telling God exactly what you're currently dealing with in your relationships, work, family, spiritual life, and decision-making, then ask Him to speak to you about these specific issues through that day's Bible passage. Write down your concerns and questions before reading so you can recognize when the scripture addresses those exact areas.

Choose one specific challenge you're currently facing and commit to seeking God's perspective on that situation through scripture for the next seven days. Each day, ask Him the same specific question about this challenge, then read your planned Bible passage looking for connections between the text and your circumstances. Keep a record of any insights, comfort, or guidance you receive related to this situation.

Obtain an Amplified Bible and select three passages that address your most common spiritual struggles or life challenges. Spend one week meditating on these three passages, reading each one slowly and paying attention to the expanded language that provides deeper insight into God's character, His promises, and His practical guidance for your circumstances. Write down amplified words and phrases that feel particularly relevant to your current needs.

Establish a maximum reading pace that allows you to actually encounter God through His word rather than just processing information quickly. Commit to reading no more than one chapter per day, focusing on quality of encounter rather than quantity of material covered. When a verse or passage feels particularly relevant to your circumstances, stop reading and spend the rest of your devotional time meditating on that specific text.

Create a scripture journal specifically for recording moments when God's word speaks directly to your circumstances. Each day, write down at least one verse that felt relevant to your current situation, along with your understanding of how it applies to your specific challenges or spiritual growth areas. Review this journal weekly to look for patterns in how God communicates with you through biblical text.

Practice responding immediately to guidance you receive through scripture by taking one specific action based on what God shows you through His word each day.

If He highlights areas where you need to grow spiritually, take concrete steps toward that growth. If He provides comfort for difficult circumstances, rest in that comfort and share it with someone else who needs encouragement. If He gives direction for decisions, follow that direction with confidence.

Identify one mature believer who demonstrates wisdom in applying scripture to daily life and ask them to pray with you about developing deeper encounter with God through His word. Share your desire to move beyond Bible study to Bible communion and ask for their accountability in maintaining consistent daily scripture meditation. Don't ask them to interpret what you think God is saying through scripture but do ask them to pray for your spiritual discernment and growth in recognizing His voice through biblical text.

Finally, commit to testing significant guidance you receive through scripture against sound biblical interpretation, internal peace, and confirmation through circumstances before making major decisions based on what you believe God has shown you through His word. Establish the practice of seeking multiple forms of confirmation when scripture seems to provide direction for important choices or changes in your life.

These practices will systematically transform your Bible reading from information gathering into personal encounter with God's presence and establish scripture as your primary means of ongoing communion with His voice throughout each day. They will teach you to recognize when God is speaking to you personally through biblical text and provide the foundation for living with constant awareness of His guidance through His written word.

God's word is alive and active, ready to speak directly to every area of your life when you learn to approach scripture as personal conversation rather than ancient literature. These steps will teach you how to position your heart for that encounter.

Chapter 4 | Developing Intimate Prayer Life

Do not be anxious or worried about anything, but in everything [every circumstance and situation] by prayer and petition with thanksgiving, continue to make your [specific] requests known to God. And the peace of God [that peace which reassures the heart] will guard your hearts and your minds in Christ Jesus.
Philippians 4:6-7 AMP

Prayer becomes intimate when you stop performing religious rituals and start having real conversations with the God who created you specifically to commune with His presence every moment of every day. Most believers treat prayer like a spiritual duty they need to fulfill rather than the natural communication that flows between people who genuinely love each other and want to share their lives together.

You've been taught to pray at God instead of praying with God, presenting your requests and concerns without creating space for His response, without listening for His perspective, and without building the kind of ongoing dialogue that characterizes intimate relationships between people who know each other deeply and care about each other's thoughts, feelings, and daily experiences.

Intimate prayer transforms your entire spiritual life because it establishes ongoing communion with God's presence that continues throughout your day rather than being confined to specific prayer times or religious settings. When you learn to pray conversationally, you discover that God wants to be involved in every decision you make, every relationship challenge you face, every work situation you encounter, and every emotion you experience throughout your normal daily activities.

This level of intimacy with God through prayer requires unlearning religious habits that create distance between you and His presence while learning communication skills that allow you to recognize His voice, sense His heart, and respond to His guidance as naturally as you would respond to conversation with your closest friend or family member.

Why Your Prayers Feel One-Sided

Your prayers feel one-sided because you've been trained to treat prayer like making requests to a distant authority figure rather than having conversations with a loving Father who wants to share His thoughts, feelings, and perspectives about your daily circumstances, relationships, and spiritual growth areas. Traditional prayer models focus on presenting your needs to God and trusting Him to respond through circumstances, other people, or general feelings of peace, but they don't teach you how to actually hear His voice during your prayer times.

Most believers pray by talking continuously throughout their entire prayer session, filling every moment with words, requests, praise, or religious phrases that leave no space for God to respond directly to what they're sharing with Him. This turns prayer into a spiritual monologue where you do all the talking and assume God will communicate back through other means at other times, but it prevents the real-time dialogue that creates intimate relationship between you and His presence.

Religious prayer culture has taught you to use formal language and spiritual vocabulary when talking to God, as if He requires you to sound religious or theologically correct before He'll listen to your concerns or respond to your questions. This formality creates emotional distance that prevents the kind of honest, vulnerable communication that builds intimate relationships between people who trust each other completely and share their real thoughts and feelings without pretense or performance.

You've also been conditioned to believe that God primarily responds to prayer through changed circumstances rather than direct communication, which means you never learn to recognize when He's actually talking back to you during your prayer times. You present your requests and then wait for external validation that He's heard you, but you miss the gentle impressions, quiet thoughts, and internal responses that represent His immediate communication about your concerns and questions.

Many believers unconsciously limit their prayers to topics they think are appropriate for God's attention, avoiding discussion of daily frustrations, relationship conflicts, work stress, or personal insecurities because they assume these concerns are too mundane for spiritual conversation. This selective sharing prevents intimate relationship because you're not bringing your whole life to God, only the parts you think He wants to hear about.

Intimate relationships require complete honesty about all areas of life, including the messy, complicated, and embarrassing parts that you might prefer to handle on your own. God wants to hear about your frustrations with difficult people, your anxiety about financial pressures, your confusion about parenting decisions, and your disappointment with circumstances that haven't worked out the way you hoped they would.

Your prayers also feel one-sided because you approach God with solutions already in mind rather than genuinely seeking His perspective on your situations. You tell Him what you want Him to do about your problems instead of asking what He thinks about your circumstances and how He wants you to respond to the challenges you're facing. This approach treats God like a cosmic vending machine that dispenses blessings when you insert the right prayers rather than a wise counselor who has insights and perspectives that could transform how you understand and handle your situations.

Religious prayer training has also created the expectation that meaningful prayer requires extended time periods and formal settings, which prevents you from developing the ongoing conversational relationship with God that continues throughout your normal daily activities. You wait for special prayer times instead of learning to commune with His presence while you're working, driving, cooking, exercising, or handling routine responsibilities.

Intimate prayer happens throughout the day as you share your thoughts and reactions with God in real time, ask for His wisdom about decisions as they arise, and include Him in your emotional responses to both positive and challenging circumstances. This ongoing dialogue creates constant awareness of His presence and involvement in every area of your life rather than limiting your relationship with Him to scheduled devotional periods.

Many believers also struggle with one-sided prayer because they unconsciously fear what God might say to them if they actually listen for His response. They worry that He might ask them to do something difficult, give up something they enjoy, or make changes they don't want to make. This fear creates internal resistance that blocks their ability to hear His voice clearly and prevents the vulnerable openness that intimate communication requires.

God knows when you're not really ready to hear His perspective, and He often waits to speak clearly until you've reached a place of genuine surrender where you want His will more than your own preferences. This doesn't mean He's withholding communication to punish you, but rather that He's waiting for you to become genuinely open to His guidance regardless of what it might require from you.

Finally, your prayers feel one-sided because you've never learned to distinguish between your own thoughts during prayer times and God's actual responses to what you're sharing with Him. When the Holy Spirit brings comfort, wisdom, or guidance to your mind during prayer, you assume you just thought of something helpful rather than recognizing that God is actively responding to your concerns and questions.

Learning to recognize God's voice during prayer requires paying attention to thoughts that feel different from your normal mental processing, ideas that provide wisdom beyond your natural understanding, and insights that address the root issues in your circumstances rather than just surface concerns. His responses during prayer typically bring peace rather than anxiety, provide practical wisdom for your specific situations, and align with biblical principles while addressing your personal circumstances.

Creating Your Secret Place with God

Your secret place with God is both a physical location where you can commune with His presence without distraction and a spiritual posture of heart that allows you to recognize His voice, sense His nearness, and respond to His guidance throughout every area of your daily life. Creating this secret place requires intentional preparation of both your external environment and your internal spiritual condition to support intimate dialogue with the God who wants to share His thoughts, feelings, and perspectives about everything that concerns you.

The physical dimension of your secret place needs to be a location where you can pray, read scripture, and listen for God's voice without interruption from other people, electronic devices, or environmental distractions that prevent focused attention on His presence. This doesn't require a large space or elaborate setup, but it does need to be a place where you can consistently meet with God at the same time each day and where your mind can quickly shift into communion mode because of the environmental cues you've established.

Choose a specific chair, corner of a room, or outdoor location that you use exclusively for prayer and scripture reading and arrange this space to minimize distractions while creating visual reminders of God's presence and faithfulness in your life. This might include a Bible, journal, and pen for recording what you sense God saying to you, along with personal items that remind you of His goodness, such as photos of answered prayers, verses that have been particularly meaningful, or symbols that represent His character and promises.

Establish consistent timing for your daily meetings with God in your secret place, choosing a time when your mind is naturally alert and your schedule is least likely to be interrupted by urgent responsibilities or other people's demands on your attention. For most people, early morning provides the best opportunity for focused communion because your mind hasn't yet become occupied with the day's tasks and concerns, but the key is consistency rather than specific timing.

Protect your secret place time by turning off all electronic devices, informing family members or roommates that you're not available during this period, and refusing to use this time for other activities even when you feel busy or stressed. Your relationship with God deserves the same priority and protection you would give to important appointments with people you love and respect.

The spiritual dimension of your secret place involves cultivating internal conditions that allow you to commune with God's presence regardless of your physical location or external circumstances. This spiritual secret place travels with you throughout your day and enables you to maintain ongoing dialogue with God while you're working, traveling, or handling routine responsibilities.

Begin developing your spiritual secret place by practicing the presence of God throughout your normal daily activities, regularly acknowledging His nearness and inviting His involvement in your thoughts, decisions, and interactions with other people. This might involve brief prayers throughout the day, asking for His wisdom about decisions as they arise, or sharing your emotional reactions to circumstances as they unfold.

Your spiritual secret place also requires learning to recognize when God is speaking to you through gentle impressions, quiet thoughts, and internal peace or unrest about different directions and decisions. This spiritual sensitivity develops through regular practice of listening prayer during your physical secret place times, but it extends into ongoing awareness of His communication throughout all your daily activities and relationships.

Cultivate expectant faith that God wants to communicate with you regularly rather than just during formal prayer times, and pay attention to thoughts that provide wisdom beyond your natural understanding, insights that address the real issues in your circumstances, and peace that comes from recognizing His guidance about decisions you need to make.

Create boundaries around your secret place by refusing to allow other activities, concerns, or relationships to intrude on your focused time with God, and by learning to redirect your attention to His presence when your mind wanders to other topics during prayer and scripture reading. This mental discipline improves with practice and becomes easier as you experience the satisfaction and peace that comes from intimate communion with His presence.

Your secret place should also include regular confession and repentance that keeps your heart clean before God and removes barriers to intimate communication that develop when you harbor unforgiveness, maintain sinful attitudes, or avoid dealing with areas where you know you need to grow spiritually. Unconfessed sin creates distance in your relationship with God that prevents the vulnerability and openness that intimate prayer requires.

Make your secret place a refuge where you can be completely honest with God about your fears, frustrations, hopes, and questions without trying to sound spiritual or hide your real thoughts and feelings. God already knows what you're thinking and feeling, and He wants authentic relationship rather than religious performance.

Use your secret place to develop consistent habits of worship and gratitude that keep your heart focused on God's goodness and faithfulness rather than being overwhelmed by your circumstances and challenges. Regular acknowledgment of His character and His blessings in your life creates the spiritual atmosphere where intimate communion flourishes and where you can hear His voice more clearly.

Finally, remember that your secret place with God is meant to be a launching pad for ongoing relationship throughout your day rather than a container that limits your communion with Him to specific times and locations. The intimacy you develop during your focused prayer times should overflow into constant awareness of His presence and regular dialogue with His voice as you navigate all the relationships, responsibilities, and decisions that fill your normal daily experience.

Moving from Requests to Relationship

Most believers approach prayer like a cosmic shopping list, presenting their requests to God and hoping He'll provide what they've asked for, but intimate prayer focuses primarily on knowing God's heart, understanding His perspective, and enjoying His presence rather than just receiving His blessings or solutions to problems. This shift from request-focused prayer to relationship-centered communion transforms your entire spiritual life because it establishes ongoing dialogue with God that continues throughout your day rather than being limited to times when you need something from Him.

Request-focused prayer treats God like a divine problem-solver who exists to make your life easier and more comfortable, while relationship-centered prayer recognizes that communion with His presence is itself the greatest blessing you could ever receive and the source of satisfaction for every spiritual hunger in your heart. When you learn to enjoy God for who He is rather than just appreciating what He does for you, prayer becomes a joy rather than a duty and creates the foundation for unshakeable peace regardless of your external circumstances.

This doesn't mean you should stop bringing your concerns and needs to God in prayer, because He genuinely cares about every area of your life and wants to provide wisdom, comfort, and practical help for all your challenges and decisions. But it does mean that your primary motivation for prayer should be desire for His presence rather than desire for His intervention, and your greatest satisfaction should come from knowing Him rather than from receiving answers to your requests.

Begin moving from requests to relationship by spending the first portion of every prayer time focused entirely on God's character, His goodness in your life, and your appreciation for His presence rather than immediately launching into your list of concerns and needs. This worship-focused beginning creates the right spiritual atmosphere for intimate communion and reminds your heart that God Himself is your greatest treasure rather than the things you hope He'll provide.

Practice talking to God about His character qualities that you've observed in scripture or experienced personally, expressing genuine appreciation for His faithfulness, wisdom, love, patience, and involvement in your daily circumstances. This kind of worship-based prayer deepens your relationship with God because it focuses your attention on who He is rather than what you want Him to do, and it creates emotional intimacy that comes from expressing genuine love and gratitude.

When you do bring your concerns and requests to God, frame them in the context of seeking His perspective rather than just asking for specific outcomes. Instead of praying "Please help me get this job," pray "What do you want me to understand about this job opportunity, and how should I approach this situation?" Instead of "Please fix my marriage," ask "How do you want me to love my spouse better, and what changes do you want to make in my heart?"

This approach invites God's wisdom about your

circumstances rather than just requesting His intervention, and it opens your heart to receive guidance that might be different from the solutions you had in mind. It also creates opportunities for God to address root issues in your heart and character that contribute to your external challenges, leading to lasting transformation rather than just temporary relief from difficult circumstances.

Spend significant portions of your prayer time simply enjoying God's presence without talking at all, sitting quietly in awareness of His nearness and allowing your heart to rest in the security of His love rather than feeling compelled to fill every moment with words or requests. This contemplative dimension of prayer builds emotional intimacy with God and teaches you to find satisfaction in communion with His presence rather than just in receiving answers to your prayers.

During these quiet times, pay attention to what you sense about God's heart toward you, His pleasure in your company, and His desire to be involved in every area of your life. Allow yourself to receive His love rather than constantly trying to earn it through spiritual performance or good behavior, and rest in the truth that He enjoys spending time with you simply because you're His beloved child.

Learn to pray conversationally by sharing your

thoughts and reactions with God throughout the day rather than saving all your communication for formal prayer times, and by asking for His perspective on situations as they arise rather than waiting until you have major problems that require His intervention. This ongoing dialogue creates constant awareness of His presence and transforms your daily experience into continuous communion with His heart.

Conversational prayer might involve asking God what He thinks about a decision you need to make, sharing your emotional reactions to challenging circumstances as they unfold, or simply acknowledging His presence during routine activities like driving, cooking, or exercising. This kind of ongoing communication builds intimacy through shared experience and keeps your heart connected to His throughout all your daily activities.

Practice listening for God's responses during your prayer times by creating space for His communication rather than filling every moment with your own words, and by paying attention to thoughts, impressions, or insights that provide wisdom beyond your natural understanding. His responses might come as gentle corrections to wrong thinking, comfort for emotional pain, guidance for difficult decisions, or simply assurance of His love and presence during challenging seasons.

When God does provide answers to your requests or intervenes in your circumstances, respond with genuine gratitude that focuses on appreciation for His character and His heart toward you rather than just relief that your problems have been solved. This kind of worship-based gratitude deepens your relationship with God and creates the spiritual foundation for continued intimacy regardless of whether future prayers receive the answers you're hoping for.

Finally, remember that the goal of relationship-centered prayer is not to eliminate all requests or to pretend you don't have real needs and concerns that require God's help. The goal is to build such intimate communion with His presence that your requests flow naturally from ongoing dialogue rather than representing the primary content of your prayer life, and to find such satisfaction in knowing God personally that you can trust His wisdom even when His answers are different from what you expected.

When Prayer Becomes Conversation

Prayer transforms from religious duty into natural conversation when you learn to recognize God's voice responding to what you share with Him and when you develop the spiritual sensitivity that allows you to distinguish His communication from your own thoughts, emotions, and mental processing. This conversational dimension of prayer creates the kind of intimate relationship with God that most believers long for but have never experienced because they've never been taught how to listen for His side of the dialogue.

Conversational prayer feels as natural and comfortable as talking with your closest friend because you've learned to recognize how God specifically communicates with you, you've developed confidence in His desire to share His thoughts and perspectives about your circumstances, and you've experienced enough of His faithful responses to trust that He's actively listening and responding even when His communication is subtle or different from what you expected.

The key to developing conversational prayer is creating space for God's responses during every prayer session and learning to pay attention to the gentle ways He typically communicates rather than expecting dramatic or obviously supernatural messages that leave no room for doubt about their divine origin. God usually speaks through quiet impressions, sudden insights, peaceful confidence about decisions, or thoughts that provide wisdom beyond your natural understanding of situations.

Begin every prayer time by acknowledging that you expect God to respond to what you're about to share with Him and that you're prepared to listen for His perspective on your circumstances, relationships, and decisions. This shift in expectation from monologue to dialogue changes the entire atmosphere of your prayer experience and positions your heart to recognize His communication when it comes.

After sharing your concerns, questions, or requests with God, sit quietly for several minutes with your attention focused on listening for His response rather than continuing to talk or moving on to other activities. During this listening time, pay attention to any thoughts, impressions, or insights that come to mind, especially those that provide perspective you hadn't considered or wisdom that goes beyond your natural understanding of the situation.

God's responses during conversational prayer typically address the heart issues behind your surface concerns rather than just providing solutions to your immediate problems. When you pray about relationship conflicts, He might show you attitudes in your own heart that need to change rather than just giving you strategies for dealing with difficult people. When you pray about financial pressures, He might address your anxiety and trust issues rather than just providing more money.

This deeper level of communication requires vulnerability and openness to receive correction, guidance, or perspective that challenges your natural thinking patterns and preferences. Conversational prayer becomes intimate when you're willing to hear God's honest assessment of your circumstances and His loving guidance about changes you need to make rather than just seeking His validation of your existing plans and preferences.

Learn to distinguish between your own thoughts during prayer times and God's actual responses by paying attention to the quality and content of different mental impressions. Your own thoughts typically reflect your existing knowledge, emotional state, and personal preferences, while God's communication often provides insight that surprises you, wisdom that goes beyond your natural understanding, and perspective that addresses root issues rather than just surface symptoms.

God's responses during prayer also typically bring peace rather than anxiety, even when His guidance involves difficult obedience or challenging changes. His communication aligns with biblical principles, demonstrates supernatural wisdom about your specific circumstances, and often includes practical steps you can take immediately rather than vague spiritual encouragement that doesn't connect to your real life.

Conversational prayer develops gradually through consistent practice rather than dramatic spiritual breakthroughs, and your ability to recognize God's voice will increase over time as you become familiar with how He specifically communicates with you. Some people sense His responses through logical thoughts and clear reasoning, others through intuitive impressions and gut feelings, and still others through scripture verses that come to mind or sudden understanding about complex situations.

Pay attention to patterns in how God speaks to you during prayer times so you can become more confident in recognizing His communication and distinguishing it from your own mental processing. Keep a prayer journal where you record both your requests and the responses you think you receive, then review these records over time to evaluate the accuracy and helpfulness of what you thought you heard from God.

Practice conversational prayer throughout your day by sharing your thoughts and reactions with God as circumstances unfold and by asking for His perspective on decisions as they arise rather than limiting your dialogue to formal prayer times. This ongoing communication creates constant awareness of His presence and transforms your daily experience into continuous communion with His heart and mind.

When prayer becomes truly conversational, you'll find that your relationship with God feels as real and satisfying as your relationships with people you love and trust completely. You'll experience the joy of sharing your life with Someone who understands you perfectly, cares about every detail of your circumstances, and provides wisdom that transforms how you handle challenges and make decisions.

Conversational prayer also creates unshakeable confidence in God's love and involvement in your life because you've experienced His personal attention and care through direct communication rather than just believing theological concepts about His character. When you know from personal experience that God listens to your concerns and responds with wisdom and comfort, your faith becomes rooted in relationship rather than just religious beliefs.

Finally, remember that conversational prayer is meant to overflow into every area of your life rather than being confined to specific prayer times or spiritual settings. The dialogue you develop with God during focused prayer sessions should continue throughout your day as you include Him in your thoughts, seek His wisdom about daily decisions, and share your emotional reactions to both positive and challenging circumstances.

Chapter 4 Call to Growth

Your prayer life will determine whether you spend the rest of your life talking at God while wondering if He's listening or learning to commune with His presence through ongoing dialogue that provides His wisdom, comfort, and guidance for every area of your daily circumstances and relationships. The specific changes you make in how you approach prayer this week will establish patterns that either increase or decrease your intimacy with God's heart and your sensitivity to His voice.

Starting tomorrow, restructure your daily prayer time to include equal portions of talking and listening by setting a timer for half your available prayer time to share your concerns with God, then setting the timer again for the remaining time to sit quietly and listen for His responses. Write down any thoughts, impressions, or insights that come to mind during your listening periods, even if you're not sure they're from God.

Choose one specific location in your home that you

will use exclusively for prayer and scripture reading, and arrange this space to minimize distractions while creating visual reminders of God's faithfulness in your life. Commit to meeting with God in this same location at the same time each day for the next thirty days, protecting this time from interruptions by turning off electronic devices and informing others that you're unavailable during this period.

Transform your request-focused prayers into relationship-centered dialogue by beginning each prayer session with five minutes of worship and gratitude focused entirely on God's character and His goodness in your life rather than immediately presenting your needs and concerns. Practice expressing genuine appreciation for who He is rather than just what He does for you.

When you do bring your concerns to God, reframe them as requests for His perspective rather than just appeals for specific outcomes. Instead of asking Him to change your circumstances, ask Him what He wants you to understand about your situation and how He wants you to respond. Write down any guidance you receive and take one specific action based on His direction each day.

Develop conversational prayer throughout your day by sharing your thoughts and reactions with God in real time rather than saving all your communication for formal prayer times. Practice asking for His wisdom about decisions as they arise, acknowledging His presence during routine activities, and including Him in your emotional responses to both positive and challenging circumstances.

Create a prayer journal where you record both your requests and the responses you think you receive from God during your listening times. Each week, review what you've written to look for patterns in how God communicates with you and to evaluate whether the guidance you thought you received has proven helpful and accurate in your actual circumstances.

Practice distinguishing between your own thoughts during prayer and God's actual responses by paying attention to impressions that provide wisdom beyond your natural understanding, bring peace rather than anxiety, and address root issues in your circumstances rather than just surface concerns. Test significant guidance against scripture, internal peace, and confirmation through circumstances before taking major action.

Finally, find one mature believer who demonstrates intimacy with God through prayer and ask them to pray with you about developing deeper conversational relationship with His presence. Share your desire to move beyond one-sided prayer to genuine dialogue and ask for their accountability in maintaining consistent daily communion with God's heart and voice.

These practices will systematically transform your prayer life from religious duty into intimate conversation with the God who created you for ongoing dialogue with His presence throughout every area of your daily experience. They will teach you to recognize His voice, trust His guidance, and find satisfaction in communion with His heart that transcends your external circumstances.

God is waiting to have real conversations with you about everything that concerns your heart. These steps will teach you how to listen for His side of the dialogue.

Chapter 5 | Experiencing God's Presence Daily

It is because of the Lord's lovingkindnesses that we are not consumed, because His [tender] compassions never fail. They are new every morning; great and beyond measure is Your faithfulness. Lamentations 3:22-23 AMP

God's presence surrounds you every moment of every day, but most believers live as if He only shows up during church services or formal prayer times because they've never learned to recognize the constant reality of His nearness in their ordinary moments, daily routines, and seemingly mundane experiences. The distance you feel from God has nothing to do with His actual location and everything to do with your awareness of where He already is.

You were created to live in continuous communion with God's presence, not just to visit with Him occasionally when you remember to pray or feel spiritually motivated. Your heart was designed to recognize His involvement in every conversation, every decision, every challenge, and every blessing that fills your normal daily experience.

When you learn to sense His presence consistently, your entire life becomes an ongoing encounter with His love, wisdom, and guidance.

The goal isn't to feel God's presence more intensely during special spiritual moments but to develop such natural awareness of His constant nearness that communing with Him becomes as automatic as breathing. You want to reach the place where His presence feels more real and reliable than your physical surroundings, where His voice becomes the steady background music of your daily experience, and where His involvement in your circumstances becomes so obvious that you wonder how you ever missed it before.

This level of spiritual awareness transforms everything about how you approach relationships, work, challenges, and decisions because you're no longer trying to handle life on your own strength while hoping God will help when things get difficult. Instead, you're living from the security of knowing that the Creator of the universe is actively involved in every detail of your circumstances and is constantly providing the wisdom, strength, and guidance you need for whatever you're facing.

Why God Feels Distant Even When You're Seeking Him

God feels distant when you're seeking Him because you're looking for His presence in dramatic spiritual experiences, obvious supernatural signs, or intense emotional encounters that confirm His nearness in ways that feel undeniably divine, but He typically reveals Himself through gentle whispers, ordinary circumstances, and quiet moments that require spiritual sensitivity to recognize rather than overwhelming displays of power that force acknowledgment of His presence.

Your expectations about how God should reveal Himself create barriers to recognizing how He actually communicates and shows up in your daily life. Church culture has trained you to associate God's presence with specific feelings, particular worship styles, or certain spiritual activities, but He's actually present and active in every moment whether you feel Him or not, whether you're in church or at work, whether you're praying or just going about your normal routine.

The problem isn't that God has moved away from you or that He only reveals Himself to certain believers who have achieved some level of spiritual maturity you haven't reached yet. The problem is that you've been conditioned to expect His presence to feel a certain way or manifest through specific experiences, and when your actual encounters with Him don't match those expectations, you assume He's not there rather than learning to recognize His more subtle forms of communication and involvement.

God often feels distant during seasons when you're trying harder to find Him because increased spiritual effort can actually create internal noise that drowns out His gentle voice and prevents the quiet receptivity that allows you to sense His nearness. When you're anxious about your spiritual state, worried about whether you're praying correctly, or frustrated about not feeling His presence, those emotions create mental and spiritual static that makes it harder to recognize His constant communication.

Your busy lifestyle also creates barriers to experiencing God's presence because constant activity, mental stimulation, and external distractions prevent the internal stillness that allows you to notice His involvement in your circumstances and His responses to your prayers. When your mind is always occupied with tasks, responsibilities, and entertainment, you don't have the mental space to recognize the gentle ways He speaks and shows up throughout your day.

God's presence often feels distant when you're going

through difficult circumstances because pain, stress, and emotional overwhelm can create spiritual numbness that blocks your ability to sense His comfort and guidance even though He's actively providing both. During challenging seasons, your natural focus shifts to problem-solving and emotional survival, which can prevent you from noticing the ways He's supporting you, speaking to you, and working in your situation.

This spiritual numbness during difficult times doesn't mean God has abandoned you or that He's less present during your struggles than during your peaceful seasons. It means your spiritual sensitivity has been temporarily affected by the emotional and mental demands of your circumstances, and you need to intentionally create space to reconnect with His presence rather than waiting for Him to break through your distraction with dramatic intervention.

Unconfessed sin and unresolved spiritual issues also create distance from God's presence because guilt, shame, and spiritual compromise affect your ability to commune with His holiness naturally and comfortably. When you know there are areas of your life that don't align with His will but you haven't dealt with them honestly, those issues create internal barriers that prevent the vulnerability and openness that intimate communion requires.

God doesn't withdraw His presence as punishment for your failures, but unaddressed sin does affect your spiritual sensitivity and your comfort level in approaching Him with confidence. The solution isn't trying harder to feel His presence while avoiding the spiritual work that needs to be done, but rather dealing honestly with whatever is creating distance in your heart so that natural communion can be restored.

Many believers also struggle to sense God's presence because they're unconsciously trying to control how He reveals Himself rather than remaining open to the ways He actually wants to communicate and show up in their lives. When you have specific expectations about how prayer should feel, how worship should affect you, or how God should respond to your circumstances, those expectations can prevent you from recognizing His actual involvement when it doesn't match your preferences.

God reveals Himself according to His wisdom about what you need and what will best serve your spiritual growth, not according to your ideas about what would feel most satisfying or convincing. Sometimes He speaks through dramatic encounters that leave no doubt about His involvement, but more often He communicates through ordinary circumstances, quiet impressions, and gentle guidance that requires faith to recognize and respond to appropriately.

Your spiritual impatience can also create feelings of distance from God because you want immediate and obvious responses to your prayers while He often works gradually through processes that develop your character and deepen your dependence on His strength rather than your own abilities. When you're focused on receiving quick answers and dramatic interventions, you might miss the subtle ways He's actually responding to your prayers and working in your circumstances.

Finally, God sometimes feels distant because you're trying to commune with His presence while maintaining spiritual independence rather than surrendering completely to His lordship over every area of your life. True intimacy with God requires wholehearted submission to His will and genuine desire for His glory above your own comfort, and when you're holding back areas of your life from His influence, that resistance affects your ability to experience the fullness of His presence.

Recognizing God in Ordinary Moments

God shows up most often in the middle of your normal daily routine rather than during special spiritual events because He wants to be part of your regular life experience, not just a weekend visitor who appears during church services or formal prayer times. Learning to recognize His presence in ordinary moments transforms your entire day into ongoing communion with His heart and makes every activity an opportunity for spiritual encounter rather than just mundane responsibility.

The conversation that provides exactly the encouragement you needed to hear, the traffic delay that prevents you from being in the wrong place at the wrong time, the unexpected solution to a problem you've been struggling with, the person who shows up with help just when you need it most, and the peace that settles over your heart during stressful circumstances are all ways God reveals His active involvement in your daily experience when you learn to recognize His hand in seemingly coincidental events.

These ordinary manifestations of God's presence require spiritual eyes to recognize because they look like natural occurrences rather than obvious miracles, but they represent His constant care and involvement in every detail of your circumstances. When you begin paying attention to the ways things work out better than you expected, doors open that you couldn't have opened yourself, and resources appear exactly when you need them, you start to see the fingerprints of God's goodness throughout your normal daily experience.

God often speaks through the people He brings into your path during routine activities like shopping, working, or running errands. The casual comment from a coworker that gives you insight about a decision you've been praying about, the encouragement from a stranger that addresses your exact emotional needs, and the question from a friend that helps you recognize an attitude that needs to change are all ways He provides guidance and comfort through ordinary human interactions.

These divine appointments don't usually feel supernatural in the moment because they happen through natural conversations and normal social interactions, but when you're paying attention to how God might be speaking through other people, you begin to notice that certain conversations address exactly what you've been thinking about, struggling with, or praying about in ways that seem too perfectly timed to be coincidental.

Practice asking God to speak to you through the people you encounter each day, then pay attention to conversations that provide unexpected wisdom, comfort, or perspective about your current circumstances. Look for patterns where multiple people mention similar themes or ideas within a short period of time, because God often confirms His communication by bringing the same message to your attention through different sources.

God's presence also shows up through the natural beauty and created world that surrounds you every day when you take time to notice His handiwork rather than rushing through your environment without paying attention to what He's placed around you. The sunrise that reminds you of His faithfulness, the flowers that demonstrate His attention to detail, and the changing seasons that reflect His creativity and power are all ways He reveals His character through the physical world He created for your enjoyment and spiritual nourishment.

Taking time to actually see and appreciate the beauty around you creates opportunities for worship and gratitude that connect your heart to God's presence throughout your normal daily activities. Even a few moments of conscious appreciation for natural beauty can shift your spiritual awareness and remind you that the God who created such magnificence is actively involved in creating beauty in your personal circumstances as well.

God frequently reveals His presence through your emotions and internal responses to circumstances when you learn to distinguish between natural emotional reactions and the peace, joy, or comfort that He provides supernaturally during challenging situations. The calm that comes over your heart when you should be anxious, the hope that rises in your spirit during discouraging circumstances, and the love you feel for difficult people are all ways His presence manifests through your emotional experience.

Pay attention to positive emotions that don't match your circumstances or that exceed what you would naturally feel based on your personality and usual emotional patterns. These supernatural emotional responses often indicate that God is providing comfort, strength, or perspective that goes beyond your natural resources and represents His active involvement in helping you handle whatever you're facing.

God also shows up through the ideas, insights, and solutions that come to mind during ordinary activities when your conscious mind is occupied with routine tasks but your spirit remains open to His communication. The breakthrough understanding about a relationship problem while you're washing dishes, the creative solution to a work challenge while you're exercising, and the clarity about a decision while you're driving are all ways He provides guidance through your normal daily routine.

These moments of sudden insight or understanding often feel like you just figured something out on your own, but when you're paying attention to how God might be speaking through your thought processes, you begin to recognize the difference between your normal reasoning and the wisdom that comes from His spirit providing perspective that goes beyond your natural understanding of situations.

Finally, God reveals His presence through the way circumstances work together for your good even when individual events seem random or unconnected. The series of events that leads to an unexpected opportunity, the way obstacles resolve themselves just when you need them to, and the timing that brings exactly the right resources or people into your life at precisely the right moment are all evidences of His active involvement in orchestrating your circumstances according to His love and wisdom.

Learning to recognize God's presence in ordinary moments requires paying attention to patterns rather than just individual events, looking for His involvement over time rather than expecting every day to contain obvious supernatural encounters. When you begin tracking how things work out in your favor, how your needs are met, and how guidance comes at exactly the right time, you develop eyes to see His constant care and involvement in every area of your daily experience.

Cultivating Continuous Awareness of His Presence

Continuous awareness of God's presence develops through intentional practices that train your spiritual attention to remain conscious of His nearness throughout your normal daily activities rather than limiting your communion with Him to specific prayer times or spiritual settings. This ongoing awareness transforms your entire day into worship and creates the foundation for constant dialogue with His heart regardless of what you're doing or where you are.

The key to developing continuous awareness is learning to acknowledge God's presence regularly throughout your day through brief moments of recognition that keep your heart connected to His without requiring extended periods of focused prayer or meditation. These acknowledgments might be as simple as saying "Thank you, God" when something goes well, asking "What do you think about this?" when facing decisions, or just pausing to remember that He's with you during routine activities.

These brief connections with God's presence

throughout your day serve as spiritual anchors that keep your heart oriented toward His involvement in your circumstances and prevent you from slipping into the mindset that you're handling life on your own strength. They create a rhythm of ongoing communion that makes His presence feel natural and accessible rather than something you have to work hard to achieve during special spiritual moments.

Practice the discipline of acknowledging God's presence at the beginning of each new activity throughout your day, taking just a few seconds to invite His involvement before starting work tasks, entering conversations, making decisions, or handling responsibilities. This simple practice creates dozens of opportunities each day to remember His nearness and include Him in your thoughts and actions rather than just hoping He'll help when things get difficult.

These brief acknowledgments don't require formal prayer language or extended time periods, just genuine recognition that God is present and interested in whatever you're about to do. You might simply think "God, I invite you into this conversation" before talking with a difficult person, or "Help me handle this well" before addressing a challenging work situation, or "Thank you for being with me" while driving to an important appointment.

Develop the habit of asking God for His perspective on situations as they arise throughout your day rather than waiting until your formal prayer time to seek His wisdom about decisions and challenges. This ongoing dialogue creates constant awareness of His involvement and transforms your daily experience into continuous communion with His heart and mind about everything that concerns you.

This conversational approach to continuous awareness might involve asking "What do you want me to learn from this?" when facing difficulties, "How do you want me to respond?" when dealing with challenging people, or "What are you doing in this situation?" when circumstances don't make sense from your limited perspective. These brief prayers keep your heart open to His guidance and remind you that He has wisdom and perspective about your circumstances that goes beyond your natural understanding.

Create environmental cues that remind you of God's presence throughout your day by placing visual reminders in locations where you spend significant time, such as verses on your computer screen, symbols in your car, or pictures that represent His faithfulness in your home or office. These physical reminders help redirect your attention to His presence when you become absorbed in tasks and responsibilities that can cause you to forget His nearness.

Use routine activities as triggers for remembering God's presence by associating specific daily actions with brief moments of spiritual awareness. You might use washing your hands as a reminder to ask for His cleansing of your heart, eating meals as opportunities for gratitude, or checking your phone as cues to check in with His spirit about your emotional and spiritual state.

These routine-based reminders help establish continuous awareness without requiring additional time in your schedule because they attach spiritual practices to activities you're already doing throughout your day. Over time, these associations become automatic and create natural rhythms of communion that keep your heart connected to God's presence without conscious effort.

Practice sensing God's presence through your physical senses by paying attention to beauty, peace, and goodness in your environment as reflections of His character and reminders of His involvement in creating the world around you. Taking a moment to appreciate natural beauty, enjoying good food as a gift from His provision, or noticing acts of kindness as expressions of His love working through other people can all serve as doorways into awareness of His presence.

This sensory awareness of God's presence helps ground your spiritual experience in the physical world He created rather than treating communion with Him as something that only happens in your mind or during religious activities. When you learn to recognize His character reflected in the goodness around you, every positive experience becomes an opportunity for worship and gratitude that connects your heart to His presence.

Cultivate the practice of sharing your emotional responses to circumstances with God in real time rather than processing your feelings independently and then reporting to Him later during prayer times. This ongoing emotional dialogue creates intimate connection with His heart and allows Him to provide comfort, perspective, and guidance exactly when you need it most rather than after you've already struggled through difficult emotions alone.

This real-time emotional sharing might involve telling God about your frustration when traffic is heavy, your anxiety when facing difficult conversations, your excitement when good things happen, or your confusion when circumstances don't make sense. This honest dialogue keeps your heart open to His involvement in every area of your experience and prevents the emotional isolation that can develop when you try to handle your feelings without His input.

Finally, remember that continuous awareness of God's presence is a skill that develops gradually through consistent practice rather than a spiritual gift that some believers have and others don't. Your ability to remain conscious of His nearness throughout your day will increase over time as you establish habits that keep your heart oriented toward His involvement in your circumstances and as you experience the peace and guidance that comes from living in ongoing communion with His presence.

When His Presence Becomes Your New Normal

God's presence becomes your new normal when awareness of His nearness feels as natural and constant as your awareness of breathing, when communion with His heart becomes the steady background reality of your daily experience rather than something you have to work to achieve during special spiritual moments. This level of spiritual awareness transforms everything about how you approach relationships, challenges, and decisions because you're living from the security of knowing that the Creator of the universe is constantly involved in every detail of your circumstances.

When His presence becomes normal, you no longer experience dramatic shifts between feeling close to God and feeling distant from Him because you've learned to recognize His constant nearness regardless of your emotional state, external circumstances, or the intensity of your spiritual experiences. His presence becomes the reliable foundation for your daily life rather than the variable that determines whether you feel spiritually strong or spiritually empty on any given day.

This consistency of spiritual awareness means you can face difficult circumstances with peace because you know God is actively involved in your situation, make decisions with confidence because you've learned to recognize His guidance, and handle relationship conflicts with love because you're drawing from His strength rather than just your natural emotional resources. His presence provides the stability that allows you to remain spiritually centered regardless of what's happening around you.

When God's presence becomes your new normal, prayer stops feeling like a scheduled appointment with Someone you visit occasionally and becomes ongoing dialogue with a constant Companion who's always available to provide wisdom, comfort, and perspective about whatever you're experiencing. You find yourself naturally sharing your thoughts and reactions with Him throughout the day because including Him in your mental and emotional processes feels more natural than trying to handle things on your own.

This conversational relationship with God's presence means you no longer have to wait for formal prayer times to receive His guidance about decisions or His comfort during difficult moments because you've learned to access His wisdom and peace in real time as circumstances unfold. His voice becomes familiar enough that you can distinguish His guidance from your own reasoning and trust His direction even when it doesn't align with your natural preferences or understanding.

Scripture reading transforms from information gathering into ongoing encounter with God's personal communication about your current circumstances because you've learned to approach His word expecting Him to speak directly to your specific situations and spiritual growth areas. Bible verses become living conversation rather than ancient text because you recognize the same voice that speaks to you during prayer times also speaking through biblical passages with perfect relevance to your daily concerns.

When His presence becomes normal, you develop what could be called spiritual peripheral vision where you naturally notice His involvement in circumstances that used to seem random or coincidental. You recognize His provision in resources that appear exactly when you need them, His protection in dangers you avoid without realizing it, and His guidance in opportunities that open at precisely the right time for your spiritual growth and His purposes.

This spiritual awareness doesn't make you super-spiritual or disconnected from normal human experience, but it does mean you live with constant recognition that God is actively involved in orchestrating your circumstances according to His love and wisdom. You can enjoy natural blessings while acknowledging their supernatural source, handle practical responsibilities while remaining aware of His guidance, and engage in human relationships while recognizing His love working through other people.

People around you begin to notice a quality of peace and confidence in your life that doesn't depend on your external circumstances because you're drawing from spiritual resources that remain constant regardless of whether things are going well or poorly from a worldly perspective. Your emotional stability and spiritual strength become testimonies to God's faithfulness that encourage other believers and attract non-believers who want to understand the source of your security.

This doesn't mean you never experience difficult emotions or challenging circumstances, but it does mean those experiences don't shake your fundamental confidence in God's love and involvement in your life because you've learned to distinguish between temporary emotional reactions and the permanent spiritual reality of His presence and care. You can feel sad about losses while remaining secure in His comfort, experience anxiety about challenges while trusting His wisdom, and face uncertainty about the future while resting in His faithfulness.

When God's presence becomes your new normal, worship becomes a natural response to recognizing His goodness throughout your day rather than something you have to generate during church services or formal spiritual activities. You find yourself spontaneously grateful for His involvement in your circumstances, naturally acknowledging His character when you see it reflected in the world around you, and automatically praising Him for His faithfulness when you recognize His provision and protection.

This ongoing worship creates a positive spiritual atmosphere in your heart that attracts more of His presence and makes it easier to recognize His voice and sense His guidance because gratitude and praise align your heart with His character and purposes. When you're living in continuous acknowledgment of His goodness, you become more sensitive to His communication and more responsive to His direction for your life.

Finally, when His presence becomes your new normal, you discover that the satisfaction and peace you've been seeking through external circumstances, human relationships, and personal achievements were available all along through intimate communion with the God who created you specifically to enjoy relationship with His presence. This spiritual fulfillment doesn't eliminate your appreciation for worldly blessings, but it does mean those blessings enhance an already satisfying life rather than trying to fill an empty heart.

Chapter 5 Call to Growth

Your daily experience of God's presence will determine whether you spend the rest of your life feeling spiritually empty between church services or learning to live in continuous communion with the God who never leaves your side and wants to be actively involved in every conversation, decision, challenge, and blessing that fills your normal daily routine. The specific practices you establish this week will create patterns that either increase or decrease your awareness of His constant nearness throughout all your circumstances and relationships.

Starting tomorrow, practice acknowledging God's presence at the beginning of each new activity throughout your day by taking three seconds to invite His involvement before starting work tasks, entering conversations, making phone calls, or handling routine responsibilities. Use simple phrases like "God, I invite you into this" or "Help me handle this well" rather than formal prayers, and notice how these brief acknowledgments affect your awareness of His nearness.

Choose five routine daily activities such as brushing your teeth, checking your phone, washing dishes, or starting your car, and use each of these activities as triggers for remembering God's presence by pausing briefly to acknowledge His nearness every time you perform these tasks. Over the next month, these routine-based reminders will establish automatic patterns of spiritual awareness that keep your heart connected to His presence without requiring additional time in your schedule.

Create a practice of asking God for His perspective on situations as they arise throughout your day by developing the habit of brief conversational prayers such as "What do you think about this?" when facing decisions, "How do you want me to respond?" when dealing with challenging people, or "What are you doing here?" when circumstances don't make sense from your limited perspective.

Place three visual reminders of God's presence in locations where you spend significant time, such as a verse on your computer screen, a symbol in your car, or a picture that represents His faithfulness in your home or office. Use these physical cues to redirect your attention to His nearness when you become absorbed in tasks and responsibilities that cause you to forget His involvement in your circumstances.

Develop the discipline of sharing your emotional responses to circumstances with God in real time by telling Him about your feelings as they arise rather than processing emotions independently and reporting to Him later during formal prayer times. Practice saying things like "God, I'm feeling anxious about this meeting" or "Thank you for this good news" or "I'm confused about this situation" as your emotions unfold throughout the day.

Keep a daily presence journal where you record at least three specific ways you recognized God's involvement in your circumstances each day, such as provision that appeared exactly when you needed it, guidance that came through conversations or circumstances, comfort during difficult moments, or beauty that reminded you of His character. Review this journal weekly to see patterns of His faithfulness and to increase your sensitivity to His ongoing activity in your life.

Practice recognizing God's voice through ordinary conversations by asking Him each morning to speak to you through the people you encounter that day, then paying attention to comments, questions, or encouragement that address exactly what you've been praying about or struggling with. Write down these instances of divine communication through human interaction to help you recognize this pattern of His guidance.

Finally, establish the practice of ending each day by spending five minutes reviewing your day with God, thanking Him for specific ways you noticed His presence, asking forgiveness for times when you forgot His nearness, and inviting His involvement in the next day's activities and decisions. This daily review helps consolidate your awareness of His involvement and prepares your heart to recognize His presence more readily the following day.

These practices will systematically develop your ability to recognize God's constant presence and transform your daily experience from spiritual isolation into ongoing communion with the God who never leaves your side and wants to be actively involved in every detail of your circumstances and relationships.

God's presence surrounds you every moment. These steps will teach you how to recognize what has always been true.

Chapter 6 | Building Unshakeable Faith

So everyone who hears these words of Mine and acts on them will be like a wise man [a farsighted, practical, and sensible man] who built his house on the rock. And the rain fell, and the floods and torrents came, and the winds blew and slammed against that house; yet it did not fall, because it had been founded on the rock. Matthew 7:24-25 AMP

Your faith becomes unshakeable when it rests on who God is rather than how you feel, when it's anchored in His unchanging character rather than your changing circumstances, and when it's built through personal encounters with His faithfulness rather than just intellectual agreement with biblical concepts. Most believers live with faith that fluctuates based on their emotions, their circumstances, and their spiritual experiences because they've never learned to distinguish between faith rooted in feelings and faith rooted in knowing God's heart.

Unshakeable faith doesn't mean you never experience doubt, fear, or confusion about your circumstances. It means those temporary emotional responses don't alter your fundamental confidence in God's love for you, His involvement in your life, and His ability to work all things together for your good according to His perfect wisdom and timing. When your faith is truly unshakeable, difficult circumstances become opportunities to experience God's strength rather than threats to your spiritual security.

This kind of rock-solid faith develops through repeated experiences of God's faithfulness in your personal circumstances that create unshakeable confidence in His character regardless of what you're facing in any given moment. When you've seen Him provide for you in impossible situations, guide you through confusing decisions, and comfort you during devastating losses, you develop faith that can't be moved by temporary challenges or apparent delays in His answers to your prayers.

Building unshakeable faith requires intentional focus on God's unchanging nature rather than your changing feelings, systematic development of your personal history with His faithfulness, and practical skills for standing firm in His promises when your circumstances seem to contradict what you know to be true about His character and His heart toward you.

Why Your Faith Gets Shaken by Circumstances

Your faith gets shaken by circumstances because you've unconsciously built it on your feelings about God rather than on God Himself, on your understanding of how He should work rather than on His actual character, and on your expectations about how faith should feel rather than on the unchanging reality of His love and faithfulness toward you. When your faith depends on positive emotions, favorable circumstances, or clear understanding of God's purposes, it will inevitably fluctuate because all these factors change regularly throughout your spiritual journey.

Circumstance-based faith treats God's love like a reward for good behavior that can be lost through failure or withdrawn during difficult seasons, rather than recognizing His love as an unchanging aspect of His character that remains constant regardless of your performance or your external situations. When you unconsciously believe that God's feelings toward you depend on your spiritual success, relationship harmony, financial stability, or physical health, any disruption in these areas creates anxiety about whether He still cares about you and wants to help you.

This performance-based approach to faith creates a constant cycle of spiritual insecurity where you feel close to God when things are going well and distant from Him when you're struggling with sin, facing difficult circumstances, or experiencing unanswered prayers. Your confidence in His love rises and falls based on external validation rather than resting on the solid foundation of His unchanging character and His demonstrated commitment to your ultimate good.

Your faith also gets shaken when you base it on your understanding of how God should respond to your prayers rather than on trust in His wisdom to provide what you actually need when you need it most. When you pray for specific outcomes and then interpret His different responses as evidence that He doesn't care about your concerns or isn't powerful enough to change your circumstances, you're measuring His faithfulness by your limited perspective rather than by His perfect knowledge of what will best serve your spiritual growth and His eternal purposes.

This expectation-based faith assumes that God's primary job is to make your life comfortable, successful, and free from difficulty, rather than recognizing that His highest priority is developing your character, deepening your dependence on His strength, and preparing you for eternal relationship with His presence. When your faith depends on God meeting your expectations rather than trusting His wisdom to exceed your expectations in ways you might not initially recognize or appreciate, disappointment becomes inevitable.

Emotion-based faith fluctuates because it depends on how you feel about God during your prayer times, worship experiences, and spiritual activities rather than on the objective reality of His character and His promises. When your confidence in God's love depends on feeling His presence during prayer, experiencing emotional responses during worship, or sensing clear guidance about your decisions, your faith becomes vulnerable to dry seasons, spiritual numbness, and times when He seems quiet or distant.

God sometimes allows seasons of emotional dryness specifically to teach you to trust His character rather than your feelings about Him, to depend on His promises rather than your spiritual experiences, and to build faith that can stand firm even when you don't sense His presence in ways that feel satisfying or convincing to your natural emotions. These seasons aren't punishment for spiritual failure but opportunities to develop mature faith that rests on who He is rather than how you feel.

Your faith gets shaken when you focus on your problems rather than on God's power, on your limitations rather than on His resources, and on your fears rather than on His promises. When difficult circumstances consume your mental and emotional energy, they can create tunnel vision that prevents you from remembering God's past faithfulness, recognizing His current involvement, or trusting His future provision. The size of your problems begins to feel larger than the size of your God.

This problem-focused perspective treats your circumstances as more real and powerful than God's ability to work in and through those circumstances for your good. When you spend more time analyzing your challenges than remembering God's character, more energy worrying about potential outcomes than trusting His wisdom, and more attention on what you lack than on His abundant resources, your faith naturally weakens because your focus determines your spiritual strength.

Finally, your faith gets shaken when you try to understand God's ways with your limited human reasoning rather than trusting His infinite wisdom even when His methods don't make sense from your perspective. When you demand logical explanations for His timing, clear understanding of His purposes, or obvious reasons for His decisions before you're willing to trust Him completely, you're essentially making your faith dependent on your ability to comprehend His infinite mind with your finite understanding.

Mature faith trusts God's heart even when you can't understand His ways, believes in His goodness even when His methods seem confusing, and rests in His love even when His timing doesn't match your preferences. This kind of faith develops through choosing to trust His character when your circumstances seem to contradict His promises and through building your confidence on His demonstrated faithfulness rather than on your ability to understand His purposes.

Developing Faith That Stands Through Storms

Faith that stands through storms is built on the bedrock of God's unchanging character rather than the shifting sand of your changing circumstances, emotions, or understanding of His purposes. This unshakeable foundation requires systematic focus on who God is according to His word and His demonstrated faithfulness rather than on how you feel about Him or how well you understand His current work in your life.

Begin building storm-proof faith by creating a personal collection of biblical truths about God's character that you can review and declare over your circumstances when your emotions or your situations tempt you to doubt His love, His power, or His involvement in your life. These character-based truths serve as anchors that keep your faith steady when the storms of life create confusion, fear, or discouragement that could otherwise shake your confidence in His goodness.

Your character-based collection might include truths such as "God is love, and His love for me never changes regardless of my circumstances," "God is all-powerful, and nothing I'm facing is too difficult for Him to handle," "God is wise, and He knows exactly what I need even when I don't understand His methods," and "God is faithful, and He has never failed to keep His promises to those who trust Him." These declarations help you stand firm on truth rather than being swept away by temporary emotions or challenging circumstances.

Practice declaring these character truths over your specific situations when you're tempted to doubt God's involvement or question His care for your circumstances. Instead of focusing on how big your problems are, focus on how big your God is. Instead of rehearsing your fears about the future, rehearse His promises about His provision and protection. Instead of analyzing why things aren't working out the way you hoped, remember that His ways are higher than your ways and His thoughts are higher than your thoughts.

Develop faith that stands through storms by building your personal history with God's faithfulness through keeping detailed records of how He has provided for you, guided you, protected you, and worked in your circumstances over time. This spiritual resume of God's past faithfulness becomes ammunition against doubt during future challenges because you have concrete evidence of His reliability that can't be shaken by temporary difficulties or apparent delays in His current responses to your prayers.

Create a faithfulness journal where you record specific instances of God's provision, protection, guidance, and comfort in your life, including both dramatic interventions and subtle ways He has worked behind the scenes to arrange circumstances for your good. Include dates, details, and your reflections on how each experience revealed aspects of His character and His heart toward you. This written record becomes a powerful tool for strengthening your faith during seasons when God seems quiet or distant.

Review your faithfulness journal regularly, especially during difficult seasons when you're tempted to doubt God's involvement in your current circumstances. Let the evidence of His past reliability remind you that He hasn't changed, His love for you hasn't diminished, and His power to work in your situation hasn't been reduced just because you can't see what He's doing right now or understand why He's allowing certain challenges.

Build storm-proof faith by learning to distinguish between God's timing and your timing, recognizing that His delays are not denials and that His methods often involve processes that develop your character while accomplishing His purposes. When you understand that God's primary goal is your spiritual growth and eternal good rather than your immediate comfort and temporal success, you can trust His timing even when it doesn't match your preferences or expectations.

Practice patience with God's timing by reminding yourself that He sees the entire picture of your life while you can only see the current moment, that He knows what you need to learn and how you need to grow while you're focused on what you want to change, and that He's working out details behind the scenes that you won't recognize until later. This eternal perspective helps you trust His delays and rest in His wisdom even when waiting feels difficult or confusing.

Strengthen your faith for storms by surrounding

yourself with other believers who demonstrate unshakeable confidence in God's character and who can remind you of His faithfulness when your own faith feels weak or confused. These spiritual relationships provide accountability for maintaining faith-based thinking rather than circumstance-based emotions, and they offer perspective from people who have experienced God's reliability in their own challenging seasons.

Seek out believers who have walked through significant trials while maintaining their trust in God's goodness, and ask them to share how they kept their faith strong during difficult circumstances. Learn from their experiences of God's faithfulness and let their testimonies strengthen your confidence that He will prove equally faithful in your own storms. Their stories become part of your arsenal against doubt and fear.

Finally, develop faith that stands through storms by practicing spiritual disciplines that keep your focus on God's character rather than your circumstances, such as worship that acknowledges His greatness regardless of your feelings, prayer that seeks His perspective rather than just presenting your concerns, and scripture meditation that reminds you of His promises and His past faithfulness to His people throughout history.

These disciplines create spiritual momentum that carries you through difficult seasons when your emotions might otherwise overwhelm your faith. When you've established habits of focusing on God's character during peaceful times, those same habits will sustain your faith during storms because your spiritual reflexes have been trained to turn toward Him rather than being consumed by your circumstances.

Moving from Doubt to Knowing

The journey from doubt to knowing happens through personal encounters with God's faithfulness that create unshakeable confidence in His love and His involvement in your life, transforming intellectual belief about His character into experiential knowledge of His heart toward you that can't be shaken by temporary circumstances or challenging seasons. Knowing goes beyond believing because it's based on your own history with God rather than just theological concepts or other people's testimonies about His goodness.

Doubt often persists in believers' hearts not because they lack information about God's character but because they haven't experienced enough personal encounters with His faithfulness to build confidence that overcomes their natural tendency to fear, worry, and question His involvement when circumstances become difficult or His responses don't match their expectations. Moving from doubt to knowing requires accumulating personal experiences of His reliability that create unshakeable confidence in His heart toward you.

Begin moving from doubt to knowing by asking God to give you specific personal experiences of His faithfulness that will build your confidence in His love and His involvement in your daily life. Don't just pray for general blessings or vague spiritual experiences but ask Him to show up in concrete ways that demonstrate His care for your particular circumstances, relationships, and concerns. These specific encounters become building blocks for unshakeable faith.

When you pray for personal encounters with God's faithfulness, be prepared to recognize His responses even when they don't look like what you expected or come through methods you didn't anticipate. God often demonstrates His faithfulness through ordinary circumstances, natural solutions to problems, and people who provide exactly what you need at precisely the right time. Learning to recognize His hand in seemingly natural events helps you build a history of His involvement that strengthens your faith.

Create opportunities for personal encounters with God's faithfulness by stepping out in obedience to His guidance even when you can't see how things will work out, trusting His provision even when your resources seem inadequate, and following His direction even when His methods don't make sense from your limited perspective. These acts of faith create situations where you can experience His reliability firsthand rather than just hearing about it from other people.

When you obey God's guidance despite your fears or confusion, you create opportunities to witness His faithfulness in ways that build unshakeable confidence in His character. Each time He proves reliable in your personal experience, your faith grows stronger and your ability to trust Him in future challenges increases. These personal encounters with His faithfulness become the foundation for knowing rather than just believing.

Move from doubt to knowing by paying careful attention to how God works in your circumstances over time, looking for patterns of His provision, protection, and guidance that reveal His consistent involvement in your life even when His methods vary from situation to situation. This requires keeping records of His faithfulness and regularly reviewing how He has worked in your past circumstances to build confidence in current and future challenges.

Document specific instances where God provided exactly what you needed when you needed it, where doors opened that you couldn't have opened yourself, where problems resolved in ways that exceeded your expectations, and where His guidance led to outcomes that were better than what you had planned. These documented experiences become evidence of His reliability that you can review when doubt tries to convince you that He doesn't care about your current circumstances.

Transform doubt into knowing by learning to distinguish between your temporary emotional responses to difficult circumstances and the permanent spiritual reality of God's unchanging love and faithfulness toward you. Emotions are valid indicators of your current state, but they're not reliable indicators of God's heart or His involvement in your situation. Knowing rests on His character rather than your feelings about Him.

Practice separating your emotional responses from your spiritual knowledge by acknowledging your feelings honestly while simultaneously declaring what you know to be true about God's character based on His word and your personal history with His faithfulness. You can feel afraid while knowing that He's your protector, feel confused while knowing that He's wise, and feel alone while knowing that He never leaves or abandons His children.

Move from doubt to knowing by developing personal intimacy with God through regular communion that allows you to experience His love directly rather than just believing theological concepts about His care for you. When you spend consistent time in His presence through prayer, scripture reading, and worship, you begin to sense His heart toward you in ways that create confidence based on relationship rather than just religious information.

This personal intimacy with God's presence provides experiential knowledge of His love that can't be shaken by circumstances because it's based on ongoing relationship rather than external validation. When you know from personal experience that God enjoys your company, delights in your growth, and cares about every detail of your life, that knowledge becomes unshakeable regardless of what challenges you face or how long you have to wait for answers to your prayers.

Finally, move from doubt to knowing by choosing to trust God's character when your circumstances seem to contradict His promises, believing His word when your experiences don't match your expectations, and resting in

His love when your feelings suggest that He's distant or uncaring. These choices to trust despite contrary evidence create opportunities for God to demonstrate His faithfulness in ways that transform doubt into unshakeable knowing.

Each time you choose to trust God's character despite challenging circumstances, you create space for Him to prove His reliability in your personal experience. These acts of faith in the face of doubt become the pathway to knowing because they position your heart to recognize His faithfulness when He demonstrates it in ways that might be different from what you expected but perfectly suited to your actual needs.

When Nothing Can Separate You from His Love

The security that comes from knowing deep in your heart that God's love for you is permanent and personal transforms everything about how you approach life's challenges, relationships, and spiritual growth because you're no longer trying to earn His approval or maintain His affection through your performance, circumstances, or spiritual success. When you truly understand that nothing can separate you from His love, you discover the freedom to be completely honest with Him about your struggles, failures, and fears without worrying that transparency will damage your relationship or reduce His care for you.

This unshakeable security in God's love doesn't develop through intellectual study of biblical verses about His character, though scripture certainly confirms this truth. It develops through personal encounters with His unconditional acceptance during seasons when you feel least deserving of His care, His faithful presence during circumstances when you've failed Him, and His gentle pursuit of your heart even when you've been distant or rebellious toward His guidance and His will for your life.

Most believers struggle with insecurity about God's love because they unconsciously treat it like human love that can be lost through disappointing behavior, withdrawn during difficult seasons, or reduced when they fail to meet expectations. This performance-based understanding of God's affection creates constant anxiety about whether you're spiritual enough, obedient enough, or faithful enough to maintain His approval and His active involvement in your circumstances.

God's love for you is not based on your spiritual performance but on His unchanging character and His decision to set His affection on you as His child. His love doesn't fluctuate based on your behavior, your circumstances, or your spiritual maturity because it flows from who He is rather than from who you are or how well you're living up to His standards. Understanding this truth intellectually is important but experiencing it personally through His faithful care during your worst moments is what creates unshakeable security.

Begin experiencing the security of God's unshakeable love by bringing your most shameful failures, deepest fears, and biggest disappointments directly to Him in prayer rather than trying to clean up your act before approaching His presence. His response to your complete honesty about your spiritual struggles and personal failures will demonstrate that His love for you doesn't depend on your ability to impress Him or maintain spiritual appearances.

When you discover that God's response to your honest confession is comfort rather than condemnation, acceptance rather than rejection, and increased intimacy rather than relational distance, you begin to experience the security that comes from knowing His love is truly unconditional. These personal encounters with His grace during your most vulnerable moments create confidence that nothing you could do or fail to do could ever separate you from His heart.

Develop security in God's permanent love by paying attention to how He continues to provide for you, guide you, and care about your daily concerns even during seasons when your spiritual life feels dry, your obedience has been inconsistent, or your faith has been weak. His continued involvement in your circumstances despite your spiritual struggles demonstrates that His care for you doesn't depend on your spiritual performance but on His unchanging commitment to your good.

Notice how God keeps working in your life even when you're not working very hard in your relationship with Him, how He continues to answer prayers even when your prayer life has been inconsistent, and how He keeps opening doors and providing opportunities even when you've been taking His blessings for granted. This evidence of His faithful love despite your unfaithful responses creates security that can't be shaken by future spiritual struggles or seasons of distance from His presence.

Experience the security of unshakeable love by testing God's heart toward you during your most difficult circumstances, when you're tempted to believe that He's punished you for past failures, abandoned you because of current struggles, or lost interest in your welfare because of delayed answers to your prayers. His faithful presence and continued care during these challenging seasons will prove that His love doesn't depend on your circumstances being favorable or your spiritual state being strong.

When you discover that God's love remains constant during your darkest valleys, most confusing seasons, and most painful losses, you develop security that can't be threatened by future difficulties because you know from personal experience that His heart toward you doesn't change based on your external circumstances or your internal spiritual condition. This security becomes the foundation for unshakeable faith that can face any challenge with confidence.

Build security in God's permanent love by remembering that His affection for you is based on His decision to adopt you as His child rather than on your ability to earn or maintain His approval through spiritual success. Just as earthly parents continue to love their children even when those children make poor choices, struggle with problems, or go through difficult seasons, your heavenly Father's love for you remains constant regardless of your spiritual ups and downs.

This parent-child understanding of God's love helps you recognize that His discipline during seasons of correction comes from His commitment to your growth rather than from anger about your failures, that His guidance during confusing circumstances flows from His desire to protect and provide for you rather than from disappointment in your choices, and that His patience during your spiritual immaturity reflects His long-term commitment to your development rather than temporary tolerance that might eventually run out.

Finally, rest in the security that nothing can separate you from God's love by choosing to believe His word about His heart toward you rather than trusting your feelings about His attitude during seasons when guilt, shame, or discouragement try to convince you that you've damaged your relationship with Him beyond repair. His love is not fragile, His commitment to you is not conditional, and His plans for your good are not dependent on your ability to avoid all spiritual failures.

When you truly understand that God's love for you is as permanent and unshakeable as His own character, you discover the freedom to approach Him with complete honesty, the confidence to trust His guidance even when it's challenging, and the security to face any circumstance knowing that you are permanently and personally loved by the Creator of the universe who has committed Himself to your ultimate good regardless of what you're currently facing or how long it takes to see His purposes fulfilled in your life.

Chapter 6 Call to Growth

Your faith will either be built on the solid foundation of God's unchanging character or remain vulnerable to being shaken by every difficult circumstance, challenging season, and unanswered prayer you encounter throughout your spiritual journey. The specific steps you take this week to anchor your confidence in who God is rather than how you feel will determine whether you develop unshakeable faith or continue to live with spiritual insecurity that fluctuates based on your external circumstances and internal emotions.

Starting tomorrow, create a personal collection of ten biblical truths about God's character that address your most common areas of doubt and fear, writing each truth in your own words and including specific scripture references that confirm these aspects of His nature. Focus on truths such as His unchanging love, His unlimited power, His perfect wisdom, His constant presence, and His faithful commitment to work all things together for your good. Review this collection daily for the next thirty days, declaring these truths over your circumstances regardless of how you feel.

Begin building your personal history with God's faithfulness by starting a written record of specific ways He has provided for you, guided you, protected you, and demonstrated His care throughout your life, including both dramatic interventions and subtle arrangements of circumstances that worked out for your benefit. Spend time this week writing down at least twenty instances of His past faithfulness, including dates and details that you can review when current circumstances tempt you to doubt His involvement in your life.

Choose one specific area where you currently struggle with doubt about God's love or His involvement in your circumstances and commit to bringing this concern to Him in daily prayer for the next week, asking Him to give you personal experiences of His faithfulness that will build your confidence in His heart toward you. Be prepared to recognize His responses even when they come through ordinary circumstances, natural solutions, or people who provide exactly what you need at the right time.

Practice separating your temporary emotional responses from permanent spiritual truth by developing the habit of acknowledging your feelings honestly while simultaneously declaring what you know to be true about

God's character. When you feel afraid, acknowledge the fear while declaring His protection. When you feel alone, acknowledge the loneliness while declaring His presence. When you feel unloved, acknowledge the pain while declaring His unchanging affection for you.

Test your security in God's unshakeable love by bringing your most shameful failures, deepest fears, and biggest disappointments directly to Him in prayer this week, paying attention to how He responds to your complete honesty about your spiritual struggles and personal weaknesses. Notice whether His response is condemnation or comfort, rejection or acceptance, distance or increased intimacy, and let His actual response build your confidence in His unconditional love.

Identify one mature believer who demonstrates unshakeable faith during difficult circumstances and ask them to share specific ways they keep their confidence in God's character strong when their emotions or situations tempt them to doubt His goodness. Learn from their practical strategies for maintaining faith-based thinking rather than circumstance-based emotions, and ask them to pray with you about developing stronger confidence in God's unchanging nature.

Establish a daily practice of reviewing God's past

faithfulness in your life by spending five minutes each evening remembering specific ways He provided for you, guided you, or demonstrated His care during that day, even if His involvement seemed subtle or natural rather than obviously supernatural. Write down these daily evidences of His faithfulness to build a growing record of His consistent involvement in your circumstances.

Finally, commit to choosing trust over doubt during one specific challenging situation you're currently facing by declaring God's character and His promises over your circumstances daily, regardless of how your emotions respond or how your situation appears to be developing. Use this situation as an opportunity to practice building faith that stands on His nature rather than your understanding, and document how He proves faithful even when His methods don't match your expectations.

These practices will systematically build your faith on the unshakeable foundation of God's character rather than the shifting sand of your circumstances and emotions, creating the kind of spiritual security that can face any challenge with confidence because you know from personal experience that nothing can separate you from His love or prevent Him from working all things together for your ultimate good.

Unshakeable faith isn't the absence of challenges but the presence of confidence in God's character that remains steady regardless of what you're facing. These steps will build that confidence through personal encounters with His faithfulness that transform doubt into knowing.

Chapter 7 | Living from the Knowing Place

Be still and know [recognize, understand] that I am God. I will be exalted among the nations, I will be exalted in the earth. Psalm 46:10 AMP

You've spent the last six chapters building the foundation for something that will transform the rest of your life: the ability to live from a place of deep spiritual knowing rather than religious hoping, personal certainty rather than borrowed faith, and unshakeable confidence in God's love rather than constant worry about whether He truly cares about your daily circumstances and eternal destiny.

Living from the Knowing Place means you no longer have to wonder if God hears your prayers because you've learned to recognize His voice responding to your concerns. You don't have to question whether He's involved in your circumstances because you've developed eyes to see His hand working in both dramatic interventions and ordinary arrangements that serve your good. You don't have to fear that His love for you depends on your spiritual performance because you've experienced His faithful care during your worst moments and your greatest failures.

This knowing place becomes the steady foundation for every decision you make, every relationship you navigate, and every challenge you face because you're no longer operating from spiritual insecurity or religious uncertainty. Instead, you're living from the confident assurance that comes from personal experience with God's character, His voice, and His heart toward you that can't be shaken by difficult circumstances or challenging seasons.

The transition from seeking the Knowing Place to living from the Knowing Place happens when these spiritual realities become so integrated into your daily experience that communing with God feels as natural as breathing, trusting His guidance becomes your automatic response to decisions, and resting in His love provides the emotional stability that allows you to face any situation with peace and confidence.

Why Knowing Changes Everything About How You Live

When you truly know that God loves you personally and permanently, you stop trying to earn His approval through spiritual performance and start living from the freedom that comes from secure relationship with Someone who delights in your company regardless of your current spiritual state or recent failures. This security transforms your approach to spiritual disciplines from religious duty into joyful communion, your response to correction from defensive resistance into grateful reception, and your attitude toward growth from anxious striving into peaceful cooperation with His work in your heart.

Knowing God's love personally changes how you handle relationships because you're no longer desperately seeking from people what only God can provide, no longer trying to control others to meet your emotional needs, and no longer devastated when human relationships disappoint you or fail to satisfy the deepest longings of your heart. When you know you are completely loved by the Creator of the universe, you can love others freely without demanding that they fill the God-shaped emptiness that only He can satisfy.

This security in God's love allows you to serve others without keeping score, forgive people without requiring them to earn your grace, and invest in relationships without demanding specific returns on your emotional investment. You can be generous with your time, energy, and resources because you're drawing from an unlimited source rather than trying to protect limited reserves. You can handle rejection, criticism, and misunderstanding with grace because your identity and worth are anchored in God's unchanging opinion of you rather than in other people's approval or appreciation.

When you know God's voice personally and consistently, you make decisions with confidence rather than anxiety because you've learned to distinguish His guidance from your own reasoning, other people's opinions, and cultural pressures that might lead you away from His best for your life. This ability to recognize His direction transforms decision-making from stressful guesswork into peaceful dialogue with Someone who knows all the factors you can't see and loves you too much to guide you toward anything that would ultimately harm your spiritual growth or eternal good.

Knowing His voice changes your approach to major life decisions such as career choices, relationship commitments, financial investments, and ministry opportunities because you can seek His specific guidance rather than just hoping your natural wisdom will lead you in the right direction. You can step into new opportunities with confidence when you sense His leading, and you can decline attractive options with peace when they don't align with His direction for your life, even when other people don't understand your choices.

This confidence in recognizing God's guidance also transforms your daily experience because you can include Him in smaller decisions throughout your day, ask for His wisdom about how to handle challenging conversations, seek His perspective on work situations, and invite His involvement in routine activities that might seem too mundane for divine attention. When you know His voice, every decision becomes an opportunity for communion rather than a burden you have to carry alone.

When you know God's faithfulness through personal experience rather than just biblical study, you face challenges with peace instead of panic because you've witnessed His reliability in your own circumstances and developed unshakeable confidence in His ability to work all things together for your good according to His perfect timing and methods. This experiential knowledge of His faithfulness creates emotional stability that doesn't depend on your circumstances being favorable or your understanding being complete.

Knowing His faithfulness personally changes how you respond to financial pressures, health concerns, relationship conflicts, and unexpected difficulties because you've seen

Him provide resources exactly when you needed them, open doors that seemed permanently closed, resolve problems that appeared impossible, and work through circumstances in ways that exceeded your expectations. These personal experiences with His reliability become the foundation for trust that can face any future challenge with confidence.

This experiential knowledge of God's faithfulness also transforms your prayer life because you're no longer just hoping He might help you but confidently expecting Him to work in your circumstances based on your personal history with His reliability. You can pray with bold faith because you know from experience that He hears you, cares about your concerns, and responds according to His wisdom and love even when His answers don't match your initial requests.

When you know God's presence as a constant reality rather than an occasional spiritual experience, you live with ongoing awareness of His nearness that provides comfort during lonely seasons, wisdom during confusing circumstances, and strength during overwhelming challenges. This continuous communion with His presence transforms ordinary moments into opportunities for worship, routine activities into partnerships with His purposes, and difficult situations into occasions for experiencing His supernatural peace and guidance.

Knowing His constant presence changes your entire emotional landscape because you're never truly alone, never without access to infinite wisdom, and never beyond the reach of unlimited love and power. This awareness doesn't eliminate all negative emotions or challenging circumstances, but it provides the spiritual resources that allow you to navigate difficulties with grace and find meaning in suffering that might otherwise feel pointless or overwhelming.

Making Decisions from Spiritual Confidence

Making decisions from spiritual confidence means you approach choices from the security of knowing you are loved, guided, and protected by God rather than from the anxiety that comes from trying to figure out life on your own wisdom while hoping you don't make mistakes that will ruin your future or disappoint the people you care about. This confidence doesn't eliminate the need for careful thought or wise counsel, but it provides the foundation of peace that allows you to seek God's guidance without the fear that drives desperate decision-making or paralyzed indecision.

Spiritual confidence in decision-making develops when you've experienced enough of God's faithful guidance to trust that He wants to direct your steps more than you want to be directed, that He cares about the details of your life more than you care about them yourself, and that His plans for your good are better than anything you could design with your limited understanding of what would truly serve your ultimate happiness and spiritual growth.

This confidence allows you to approach decisions as opportunities for communion with God rather than burdens you have to carry alone, tests you might fail, or problems you have to solve without adequate information. When you know that God delights in providing wisdom to His children and that He's more invested in your success than you are, decision-making becomes a collaborative process with Someone who has perfect knowledge of all the factors you can't see and unlimited power to arrange circumstances for your benefit.

Begin making decisions from spiritual confidence by bringing every choice to God in prayer before seeking advice from other people, researching your options, or analyzing the pros and cons with your natural reasoning. This doesn't mean you skip human wisdom or ignore practical considerations, but it means you start with spiritual foundation rather than treating prayer as a last resort when your own resources prove inadequate for complex decisions.

When you approach God first with your decisions, you position your heart to receive His perspective before your mind becomes fixed on particular options, or your emotions become attached to specific outcomes. This spiritual foundation helps you evaluate human advice, practical considerations, and natural preferences through the filter of His guidance rather than trying to fit His will into decisions you've already made based on limited human wisdom.

Practice making decisions from spiritual confidence by asking God specific questions about your choices rather than just presenting Him with your preferred option and hoping He'll bless your plans. Instead of praying "God, please help me get this job," ask "What do you want me to understand about this opportunity, and how does it fit with your plans for my life?" Instead of "Please make this relationship work," ask "How do you want me to approach this relationship, and what do you want me to learn through this situation?"

These specific questions invite God's wisdom about your circumstances rather than just requesting His endorsement of your preferences, and they create opportunities for Him to provide guidance that might be different from what you initially wanted but perfectly suited to what you actually need for your spiritual growth and His purposes for your life.

Make decisions from spiritual confidence by learning to distinguish between open doors that God is providing and opportunities that simply appeal to your natural desires or seem attractive from a worldly perspective. Divine opportunities typically come with internal peace that persists even when the choice involves challenge or sacrifice, align with biblical principles and your spiritual growth, and contribute to God's purposes rather than just your personal comfort or success.

When God opens doors, you'll often notice that multiple factors align in ways that seem too coordinated to be coincidental: the right people appear with the right information at the right time, resources become available exactly when you need them, obstacles that seemed impossible suddenly resolve themselves, and circumstances work together in ways that exceed what you could have arranged through your own efforts.

But not every open door represents God's will for your life, and not every closed door means He's saying no to your desires. Sometimes He closes doors to protect you from situations that would harm your spiritual growth or derail His plans for your future. Sometimes He opens doors as tests to see whether you'll choose His will over your own preferences. Learning to discern which opportunities represent His guidance requires combining attention to external circumstances with internal peace and confirmation through scripture and prayer.

Develop confidence in spiritual decision-making by starting with smaller choices that allow you to practice recognizing God's guidance without the pressure of life-altering consequences. Ask for His wisdom about daily decisions such as how to respond to difficult people, how to prioritize your time, how to handle work challenges, or how to serve your family better. These smaller opportunities to seek and follow His guidance build your confidence in recognizing His voice and trusting His direction for bigger decisions.

When you consistently experience God's faithfulness in guiding smaller decisions, you develop the spiritual confidence that allows you to trust His guidance for major choices such as career changes, relationship commitments, financial investments, or ministry opportunities. The skills you develop in recognizing His voice and following His direction in everyday situations become the foundation for confident decision-making in life-changing circumstances.

Make decisions from spiritual confidence by refusing to be pressured into choices by other people's timelines, expectations, or opinions when you haven't yet received clear guidance from God about the direction you should take. His timing is perfect, and He's capable of arranging circumstances to accommodate His will for your life even when other people think you're taking too long to decide or missing opportunities by waiting for His direction.

This doesn't mean you should use "waiting for God's guidance" as an excuse for indecision when He's already provided clear direction through His word, circumstances, or previous guidance. But it does mean you have permission to take the time you need to seek His wisdom and receive His peace about important choices rather than making decisions based on external pressure or internal anxiety about missing deadlines or disappointing people.

Finally, make decisions from spiritual confidence by remembering that God's grace covers your mistakes and that His plans for your good are not derailed by imperfect choices made with sincere hearts that sought His guidance. Even when you misunderstand His direction or make decisions that don't work out as you hoped, He's able to work through your failures and redirect your path in ways that ultimately serve His purposes and your spiritual growth.

This security in God's grace allows you to make decisions with confidence rather than paralyzed fear of making mistakes, knowing that He's more committed to your success than you are and more capable of working through your imperfect choices than you are of making perfect decisions with your limited wisdom and understanding.

Maintaining Your Knowing Place

Maintaining your knowing place requires intentional spiritual disciplines and heart attitudes that keep you connected to God's presence, sensitive to His voice, and confident in His love even during busy seasons, challenging circumstances, or times when your emotions might tempt you to doubt what you know to be true about His character and His heart toward you. The Knowing Place isn't a spiritual achievement you reach once and keep forever, but a living relationship that needs daily attention and consistent cultivation to remain strong and vibrant.

The greatest threat to maintaining your knowing place isn't dramatic spiritual failure or obvious rebellion against God's will, but the subtle drift that happens when you gradually replace personal communion with religious activity, when you start depending on other people's spiritual experiences instead of cultivating your own encounters with God's presence, or when you become so busy with good things that you don't have time for the best thing: intimate relationship with the One who created you for ongoing dialogue with His heart.

This drift away from the Knowing Place often happens so gradually that you don't notice it until you realize you've been operating from spiritual memory rather than current communion, making decisions based on past guidance rather than present direction, and drawing from previous encounters with God's love rather than fresh experiences of His care and involvement in your daily circumstances.

Maintain your knowing place by protecting your daily time with God as the non-negotiable foundation for everything else in your schedule, refusing to sacrifice intimate communion with His presence for other activities no matter how important they seem or how much pressure you feel to use that time for other purposes. This daily appointment with God isn't just another spiritual discipline to fulfill but the lifeline that keeps your heart connected to the source of everything you need for spiritual strength, emotional stability, and practical wisdom.

When you begin to view your daily time with God as optional or when you start cutting it short to accommodate other responsibilities, you're beginning the drift away from the Knowing Place toward religious activity that lacks the power and intimacy you've learned to treasure. Your relationship with God, like any meaningful relationship, requires consistent time and attention to remain vibrant and growing rather than becoming stale or distant.

Protect your knowing place by regularly evaluating your spiritual practices to ensure they're still creating genuine encounter with God's presence rather than just fulfilling religious obligations or maintaining spiritual appearances. When prayer becomes routine recitation rather than conversational dialogue, when scripture reading becomes information gathering rather than personal encounter, or when worship becomes performance rather than authentic expression of your heart toward God, it's time to refresh your approach and rediscover the intimacy that drew you into the Knowing Place.

This evaluation isn't about condemning yourself for spiritual dryness or feeling guilty about seasons when communion with God feels more difficult, but about honestly assessing whether your spiritual practices are still serving their intended purpose of connecting your heart with His presence. Sometimes maintaining your knowing place requires changing your methods while preserving your heart attitude of seeking intimate relationship with God above all other spiritual goals.

Maintain your knowing place by continuing to bring your real life to God rather than just the parts you think are appropriate for spiritual conversation, and by refusing to develop separate compartments where you handle some areas with His guidance while managing others through your own wisdom or other people's advice. The Knowing Place encompasses every area of your life and maintaining it requires ongoing integration of His presence into all your relationships, decisions, challenges, and daily activities.

When you start handling work stress without including God in your emotional processing, making financial decisions without seeking His wisdom, or managing relationship conflicts without asking for His perspective, you're creating distance from the Knowing Place by treating Him as a part-time consultant rather than a constant companion who wants to be involved in every detail of your experience.

Cultivate long-term spiritual friendships with other believers who share your hunger for intimate relationship with God and who can encourage your continued growth in recognizing His voice, sensing His presence, and trusting His guidance. These relationships provide accountability for maintaining the Knowing Place and offer perspective from people who understand the value of what you've discovered and won't try to convince you to settle for surface-level Christianity.

Spiritual friendships that support your knowing place are characterized by conversations that go beyond discussing circumstances to exploring what God is saying through those circumstances, prayer times that include listening for His voice rather than just presenting requests, and encouragement that points you toward deeper intimacy with Jesus rather than just temporary comfort for current challenges.

Maintain your knowing place by regularly sharing with others what God is teaching you, how He's speaking to you, and what you're learning about His character through your ongoing communion with His presence. This sharing serves multiple purposes: it helps you process and remember your encounters with God, it encourages other believers in their own spiritual journeys, and it creates accountability for continuing to seek fresh experiences of His faithfulness rather than coasting on past spiritual victories.

When you stop talking about what God is currently doing in your life and start only referring to past experiences of His goodness, it often indicates that you're drifting from the Knowing Place toward spiritual memory rather than living relationship. Fresh testimonies of His current involvement in your circumstances are signs of maintained intimacy with His presence.

Protect your knowing place by refusing to allow discouragement, disappointment, or spiritual dryness to convince you that you've lost what you once had or that intimate relationship with God is only available during certain seasons of life. The Knowing Place isn't dependent on your feelings, your circumstances, or your spiritual performance, but on God's unchanging character and His permanent commitment to relationship with His children.

During challenging seasons when communion with God feels more difficult or when His voice seems less clear than you've grown accustomed to experiencing, maintain your knowing place by continuing the practices that originally brought you into intimate relationship with His presence while trusting that He's still present and active even when you can't sense His involvement as clearly as you'd like.

Finally, maintain your knowing place by remembering

that it's not a spiritual destination you reach but a way of living that requires ongoing choice to prioritize relationship with God above all other pursuits, to seek His presence above all other experiences, and to value His approval above all other opinions. The Knowing Place is maintained through daily decisions to commune with His heart, trust His guidance, and rest in His love regardless of what else is competing for your attention or affection.

Becoming Someone Who Knows They Know

Becoming someone who knows they know represents the transformation from a believer who hopes God loves them to someone who lives from the unshakeable confidence that they are personally and permanently loved by the Creator of the universe, from someone who wonders if God hears their prayers to someone who expects His response because they've learned to recognize His voice, and from someone who tries to figure out life on their own while hoping for divine help to someone who naturally includes God in every decision because ongoing dialogue with His wisdom has become their normal way of approaching choices.

This identity shift from seeking to knowing doesn't

happen through a single spiritual experience or dramatic encounter with God's presence, but through the accumulation of personal encounters with His faithfulness that create such deep confidence in His character and His heart toward you that doubt becomes the exception rather than the rule in your spiritual experience. When you know that you know, challenging circumstances become opportunities to experience God's strength rather than threats to your spiritual security.

Someone who knows they know approaches prayer with expectant confidence rather than desperate hope because they've experienced enough of God's faithful responses to trust that He hears them, cares about their concerns, and will provide exactly what they need when they need it most, even when His answers don't match their initial requests or His timing doesn't align with their preferences.

This confidence in prayer doesn't mean you always get what you ask for or that God responds according to your timeline and methods, but it means you approach Him with the security that comes from knowing you're talking to Someone who loves you completely, understands your circumstances perfectly, and has unlimited power to work in your situation for your ultimate good and His eternal purposes.

When you know that you know, you make decisions with peace rather than anxiety because you've developed such familiarity with God's voice and His ways that recognizing His guidance feels as natural as recognizing a close friend's voice in a crowded room. This doesn't mean every decision becomes obvious or that you never need time to seek His wisdom, but it means you have confidence that He wants to guide you and that you can distinguish His direction from your own reasoning or other people's opinions.

This decision-making confidence allows you to step into new opportunities with faith when you sense His leading, decline attractive options with peace when they don't align with His direction, and wait patiently for His timing when the next step isn't yet clear. You can handle other people's confusion or criticism about your choices because you're more concerned with His approval than with human understanding of your decisions.

Someone who knows they know faces challenges with spiritual stability that doesn't depend on circumstances being favorable or understanding being complete because they've experienced enough of God's faithfulness during previous difficulties to trust His involvement even when they can't see what He's doing or understand why He's allowing certain struggles. This doesn't eliminate all fear or confusion during hard times, but it provides the foundation of confidence that allows you to rest in His character when His methods don't make sense.

This stability during storms comes from having a personal history with God's reliability that can't be shaken by current circumstances because it's based on repeated experiences of His provision, protection, and guidance that have proven His commitment to your good regardless of how challenging your immediate situation might appear. When you know that you know, your faith rests on who God is rather than on how you feel or what you can see happening in your circumstances.

Becoming someone who knows they know also means you live with ongoing awareness of God's presence that makes communion with His heart feel as natural as breathing, where acknowledging His involvement in your circumstances becomes automatic rather than something you have to remember to do, and where sensing His nearness provides constant comfort and guidance throughout your daily activities and relationships.

This continuous awareness of His presence doesn't mean you feel emotionally elevated all the time or that every moment feels spiritually intense, but it means you live with the settled knowledge that you're never alone, never without access to infinite wisdom, and never beyond the reach of unlimited love and power that are actively involved in every detail of your life.

When you know that you know, you approach relationships from the security of being completely loved by God rather than trying to get from people what only He can provide, which allows you to love others freely without demanding that they meet your deepest emotional needs or provide the validation that comes from knowing you're treasured by your Creator. This security transforms your relationships because you can serve without keeping score, forgive without requiring people to earn your grace, and invest emotionally without demanding specific returns.

This relational freedom comes from having your deepest needs for love, acceptance, and significance met through intimate relationship with God, which allows human relationships to be sources of joy and growth rather than desperate attempts to fill the emptiness that only He can satisfy. When you know you're loved by the One whose opinion matters most, you can handle human rejection, criticism, or misunderstanding with grace because your identity and worth are anchored in His unchanging heart toward you.

Someone who knows they know also becomes a source of spiritual strength and encouragement for other believers because they carry the confidence that comes from personal encounter with God's faithfulness, and their testimony of His reliability provides hope for people who are still learning to trust His character and recognize His voice. Your settled confidence in God's love and involvement becomes a gift to others who are seeking the same intimacy you've discovered.

This doesn't mean you become spiritually proud or that you stop growing in your relationship with God, but it means you've moved beyond the constant spiritual insecurity that characterizes believers who are still wondering if God really cares about them personally. Your confidence becomes a foundation for continued growth rather than a barrier to deeper intimacy, and your security in His love creates space for Him to challenge you toward greater maturity without threatening your sense of acceptance and belonging.

Finally, becoming someone who knows they know means you've developed such deep roots in God's character and such consistent experience of His faithfulness that your spiritual life has stability that can weather any storm, face any challenge, and maintain hope in any circumstance because you're drawing from a source that never runs dry and trusting in Someone whose love never fails and whose plans for your good never change regardless of what you're currently facing or how long you have to wait to see His purposes fulfilled.

Chapter 7 Call to Growth

Your decision to live from the Knowing Place rather than returning to spiritual uncertainty will determine whether the intimacy with God you've developed over these past weeks becomes the foundation for a lifetime of unshakeable faith or remains just a temporary spiritual experience that fades when life gets busy or challenging. The specific commitments you make today will establish whether you continue growing in confidence that you are known and loved by God or drift back into the religious routine that left you spiritually hungry in the first place.

Create a written plan for maintaining daily communion with God that includes specific times for prayer, scripture reading, and listening for His voice that you will protect regardless of how busy your schedule becomes or how many other demands compete for your attention. Write down exactly when you will meet with

God each day, where you will have these appointments, and what you will do if circumstances try to interfere with these non-negotiable times of intimate relationship with His presence.

This written plan should include backup options for maintaining communion with God during travel, illness, or unusually busy seasons, because the enemy of your soul will use any disruption in your routine to convince you that intimate relationship with God is only possible under ideal circumstances. Your plan needs to be flexible enough to adapt to changing situations while remaining firm enough to ensure that nothing prevents your ongoing dialogue with His heart.

Identify three specific areas of your life where you will practice making decisions from spiritual confidence rather than human reasoning alone, committing to seek God's guidance first in these areas and to wait for His peace before taking action even when other people pressure you to decide quickly or criticize you for taking time to pray about your choices. Choose areas such as career decisions, relationship choices, financial investments, or ministry opportunities where you can practice trusting His wisdom over your natural understanding.

Write down the specific questions you will ask God

about these decision areas and commit to spending focused time in prayer seeking His perspective before researching options, asking for human advice, or analyzing pros and cons with your natural reasoning. This practice of seeking spiritual foundation first will build your confidence in recognizing His guidance and strengthen your ability to distinguish His voice from other influences that might lead you away from His best for your life.

Establish accountability with one mature believer who shares your hunger for intimate relationship with God and who will encourage your continued growth in the Knowing Place rather than trying to convince you to settle for surface-level Christianity. Meet with this person monthly to share what God is teaching you, how He's speaking to you, and what challenges you're facing in maintaining ongoing communion with His presence.

This accountability relationship should include honest discussion about areas where you're tempted to drift from the Knowing Place, practical strategies for maintaining spiritual intimacy during busy seasons, and prayer support for continued growth in recognizing God's voice and trusting His guidance. Choose someone who demonstrates the kind of spiritual maturity you want to develop and who can provide perspective when your emotions or circumstances tempt you to doubt what you know to be true about God's character.

Create a personal testimony of your journey into the Knowing Place that you can share with other believers who are seeking deeper intimacy with God, including specific examples of how you learned to recognize His voice, sense His presence, and trust His guidance in practical situations. Write down the key turning points in your spiritual growth and the practices that were most helpful in developing ongoing communion with God's heart.

This testimony serves multiple purposes: it helps you remember and appreciate what God has done in your spiritual life, it provides encouragement for other believers who want to develop similar intimacy with His presence, and it creates accountability for continuing to seek fresh experiences of His faithfulness rather than coasting on past spiritual victories. Plan to share this testimony with at least three people in the next month.

Develop a plan for continued spiritual growth that includes specific goals for deepening your relationship with God over the next year, such as learning new spiritual disciplines, studying particular aspects of His character, or developing greater sensitivity to His voice in specific areas of your life. Write down concrete steps you will take to continue growing in spiritual maturity rather than assuming that reaching the Knowing Place means your spiritual development is complete.

This growth plan should include regular evaluation of your spiritual practices to ensure they're still creating genuine encounter with God's presence rather than becoming routine religious activities, along with specific ways you will challenge yourself to trust His guidance in new areas and rely on His strength for greater levels of obedience and service.

Finally, commit to protecting the Knowing Place by refusing to allow discouragement, disappointment, or spiritual dryness to convince you that you've lost the intimacy with God you've developed or that deep relationship with His presence is only available during certain seasons of life. Write down specific truths about God's character and His love for you that you will declare over your circumstances when emotions or situations tempt you to doubt what you know to be true about His heart toward you.

These truths should be based on your personal experiences of His faithfulness rather than just theological concepts, and they should address the specific areas where you're most likely to struggle with doubt or insecurity.

Review and declare these truths daily, especially during challenging seasons when maintaining your confidence in His love requires intentional choice rather than natural feeling.

Living from the Knowing Place is not a spiritual achievement but a way of life that requires daily choice to prioritize relationship with God above all other pursuits and to trust His character above all other voices competing for your attention and allegiance. These commitments will establish the foundation for a lifetime of unshakeable faith rooted in personal knowledge of the God who created you for intimate communion with His presence and who delights in your company more than you could ever imagine.

You have tasted and seen that the Lord is good. Now choose to live from that knowing place for the rest of your life.

The Resolve

You've Crossed the Bridge from Acknowledging to Knowing

Something fundamental has shifted in your heart over the course of this devotional that can never be undone, never be taken away, and never be reduced back to the shallow Christianity that once left you spiritually hungry and emotionally empty. You began this journey as someone who believed God existed but wondered if He truly cared about your daily concerns, someone who read about His love but wasn't sure you felt it personally, someone who prayed but wasn't confident He was listening or responding to your specific circumstances and needs.

You are no longer that person.

The bridge you've crossed from acknowledging God's existence to knowing Him personally represents the most important transformation that can happen in any believer's spiritual life, because it moves you from secondhand faith based on other people's experiences to firsthand relationship built on your own encounters with His presence, His voice, and His faithful involvement in every detail of your circumstances.

You now know what it feels like to pray and sense God's response, to read scripture and hear His personal communication about your current situations, to face challenges with the confidence that comes from recognizing His guidance, and to rest in love that you've experienced rather than just heard about from other believers or read about in books that describe what intimate relationship with Jesus should feel like.

This knowing changes everything about how you approach life because you're no longer operating from spiritual uncertainty or religious hope. You're living from the settled confidence that comes from personal experience with God's character, repeated encounters with His faithfulness, and ongoing dialogue with His heart that has become as natural and reliable as your next breath.

The spiritual hunger that drove you to seek something deeper than surface-level Christianity has been satisfied not through more religious activity or better Bible study materials, but through discovering what you were actually hungry for all along: personal, intimate, daily communion with the living God who created you specifically to enjoy relationship with His presence and who has been waiting for you to learn how to recognize His constant nearness and ongoing communication.

You've learned to distinguish between your own thoughts and God's gentle responses during prayer times. You've developed the ability to sense His presence throughout your normal daily activities rather than only during formal spiritual settings. You've experienced His personal communication through scripture that addresses your specific circumstances with supernatural timing and perfect relevance. You've discovered that He cares about every detail of your life and wants to be involved in every decision, every relationship challenge, and every area where you need wisdom or comfort.

Most importantly, you've built your own personal history with God's faithfulness that creates unshakeable confidence in His love for you, His involvement in your circumstances, and His commitment to work all things together for your good regardless of how challenging your immediate situation might appear or how long you have to wait to see His purposes fulfilled in your life.

This personal history with His reliability can never be taken away from you by difficult circumstances, challenging seasons, or other people's opinions about your spiritual experiences. You know what you know because you've experienced it personally, and that experiential knowledge becomes the foundation for unshakeable faith that can face any future challenge with confidence.

The Knowing Place you've discovered isn't just a temporary spiritual high that will fade when life gets busy or difficult. It's a new way of living that integrates intimate relationship with God into every area of your daily experience, creating ongoing communion with His presence that provides wisdom for decisions, comfort for challenges, and strength for whatever circumstances you encounter.

You've crossed a bridge that leads to a completely different quality of spiritual life than what you experienced before, and there's no going back to the spiritual emptiness and religious routine that once characterized your relationship with God. You've tasted and seen that the Lord is good in ways that create permanent hunger for continued intimacy with His presence rather than satisfaction with shallow Christianity.

Your New Life Starts Now

Your new life as someone who lives from the Knowing Place rather than religious uncertainty begins today, not someday in the future when you feel more spiritually mature or when your circumstances become more favorable for maintaining intimate relationship with God's presence. The tools you've developed for recognizing

His voice, sensing His presence, and trusting His guidance are ready to be applied to every area of your daily experience, every relationship you navigate, and every decision you face from this moment forward.

This new life doesn't require perfect spiritual performance or flawless obedience to maintain, because it's built on God's unchanging character rather than your changing spiritual state. The intimacy with His presence that you've discovered will continue to grow and deepen as you apply what you've learned to new situations, challenges, and opportunities that provide fresh context for experiencing His faithfulness and recognizing His involvement in your circumstances.

Your new life includes the confidence to make decisions based on God's guidance rather than just human wisdom, because you've learned to distinguish His voice from your own reasoning and you've experienced His faithful direction in ways that build trust in His wisdom even when His methods don't align with your natural preferences or understanding. You can step into opportunities with peace when you sense His leading, decline attractive options without regret when they don't match His direction, and wait patiently for His timing when the next step isn't yet clear.

You now have the spiritual tools to maintain ongoing dialogue with God throughout your day rather than limiting your communion with His presence to formal prayer times or religious settings. The conversational relationship you've developed allows you to include Him in your thoughts as circumstances unfold, seek His perspective on challenges as they arise, and share your emotional responses to both positive and difficult experiences in real time rather than processing everything independently and reporting to Him later.

This ongoing dialogue transforms your entire daily experience into continuous worship and creates the foundation for living with constant awareness of His nearness, His care, and His active involvement in orchestrating your circumstances according to His love and wisdom. You no longer have to wonder if God is present or if He cares about your concerns because you've learned to recognize the evidence of His involvement that surrounds you every day.

Your new life includes the ability to approach challenges with spiritual stability that doesn't depend on circumstances being favorable or understanding being complete, because you've built personal confidence in God's character through repeated experiences of His faithfulness that create unshakeable trust in His heart toward you. Difficult situations become opportunities to experience His strength rather than threats to your spiritual security.

You've developed the spiritual foundation that allows you to face uncertainty with peace, handle relationship conflicts with love drawn from His unlimited resources, and navigate financial pressures, health concerns, or work challenges with confidence in His provision and guidance rather than anxiety about outcomes you can't control through your own efforts.

Your new life also includes freedom from the spiritual insecurity that once made you question whether God truly loved you personally or whether His care for you depended on your spiritual performance. You now know from personal experience that His love is permanent and unconditional, that His commitment to your good is unshakeable, and that His plans for your life are motivated by His heart toward you rather than by your ability to earn His approval through religious activity or moral behavior.

This security in His love allows you to approach Him with complete honesty about your struggles, failures, and fears without worrying that transparency will damage your relationship or reduce His care for you. You can receive

His correction with gratitude rather than defensiveness because you know it comes from His commitment to your growth rather than disappointment in your performance.

The spiritual disciplines you've developed throughout this devotional, have become natural parts of your daily routine rather than religious duties you fulfill to maintain God's approval. Prayer feels like conversation with a close friend, scripture reading provides ongoing encounter with His personal communication, and worship flows naturally from recognition of His goodness in your circumstances rather than being something you must generate during church services.

Your new life includes the joy of sharing what you've discovered with other believers who are seeking the same intimacy with God's presence that you've found, and your testimony of His faithfulness becomes encouragement for people who are still learning to recognize His voice and trust His character. The confidence you carry becomes a gift to others who need to see evidence that deep relationship with Jesus is possible and worth pursuing.

Most importantly, your new life is characterized by settled peace that comes from knowing you are completely known and unconditionally loved by the Creator of the universe, who delights in your company and wants to be involved in every detail of your experience. This peace provides the foundation for facing any future challenge with confidence because you're drawing from a source that never runs dry and trusting in Someone whose love never fails.

Your Step-by-Step Guide to Keep Growing

Maintaining and deepening your relationship with God requires the same intentional commitment that any meaningful relationship demands, along with specific practices that keep your heart connected to His presence and your spiritual ears tuned to His voice even when life becomes busy, circumstances become challenging, or your emotions tempt you to doubt what you know to be true about His character and His heart toward you.

Continue your daily scripture communion by approaching God's word each morning with specific questions about your current circumstances and asking the Holy Spirit to speak to you personally through biblical text about the decisions you're facing, the relationships you're navigating, and the spiritual growth areas where you need His guidance and encouragement. This transforms Bible reading from information gathering into ongoing conversation with His presence that provides exactly the wisdom you need for each day's challenges and opportunities.

Read slowly enough to actually encounter God through His word rather than just processing information quickly, and when a verse or passage feels particularly relevant to your current situation, stop reading and spend time meditating on that specific text rather than continuing through your planned reading schedule. The goal is quality of encounter with His voice rather than quantity of material covered, and one verse that speaks directly to your heart provides more spiritual nourishment than entire chapters read without personal application.

Keep a scripture journal where you record passages that feel particularly meaningful, insights that provide new perspective on your circumstances, and specific ways you sense God guiding you through His written word. Review this journal regularly to see patterns in how He communicates with you through biblical text and to remember His faithful guidance during previous seasons when you needed His direction or comfort.

Maintain your listening prayer practice by continuing to create space for God's responses during every prayer session rather than filling all your time with talking, and by paying attention to thoughts, impressions, or insights that provide wisdom beyond your natural understanding of situations. His responses might come as gentle corrections to wrong thinking, comfort for emotional pain, guidance for difficult decisions, or simply assurance of His love and presence during challenging seasons.

Write down what you sense during your listening times even if you're not completely sure it's from God, because this practice helps you remember His communication and allows you to evaluate over time whether the guidance you thought you received proves helpful and accurate in your actual circumstances. Your ability to recognize His voice will continue to improve through consistent practice and honest evaluation of the results.

Ask God specific questions during your prayer times rather than just sharing general concerns, because specific questions invite specific answers that you can recognize and apply immediately to your daily life. Instead of praying about your job situation in general terms, ask Him what specific steps you should take to improve your work relationships or how He wants you to handle particular challenges you're facing with supervisors or coworkers.

Develop your presence awareness by continuing to acknowledge God's nearness throughout your daily activities through brief moments of recognition that keep your heart connected to His without requiring extended periods of focused prayer. These might be simple thoughts like "Thank you, God" when something goes well, "Help me handle this wisely" when facing challenges, or just pausing to remember that He's with you during routine activities.

Practice asking for His perspective on situations as they arise throughout your day rather than waiting until your formal prayer time to seek His wisdom about decisions and challenges. This ongoing dialogue creates constant awareness of His involvement and transforms your daily experience into continuous communion with His heart and mind about everything that concerns you.

Use routine activities as triggers for remembering His presence by associating specific daily actions with brief moments of spiritual awareness, such as using your morning coffee as a reminder to thank Him for His provision, checking your phone as a cue to check in with His spirit about your emotional state, or washing your hands as a prompt to ask for His cleansing of your heart from attitudes that don't reflect His character.

Build your spiritual confidence by continuing to act on the guidance you receive from God rather than just appreciating His wisdom without taking practical steps to follow His direction. When He shows you areas where you need to grow spiritually, take concrete action toward that growth. When He provides comfort for difficult circumstances, rest in that comfort and share it with others who need encouragement. When He gives you direction for decisions, follow that guidance with obedience even when it doesn't align with your natural preferences.

Your responsiveness to His guidance directly impacts how clearly you continue to hear His voice and how specifically He provides direction for future decisions. The Holy Spirit gives more detailed guidance to believers who consistently act on what they receive rather than just collecting spiritual insights without practical application.

Protect your knowing place by surrounding yourself with believers who share your hunger for intimate relationship with God and who encourage your continued growth in recognizing His voice and trusting His guidance rather than trying to convince you to settle for surface-level Christianity that focuses on religious activity rather than personal encounter with His presence.

Seek spiritual friendships characterized by discussions that explore what God is saying through circumstances rather than just discussing events themselves, prayer times that include listening for His voice rather than just presenting requests, and encouragement that points you toward deeper intimacy with Jesus rather than just temporary comfort for current challenges.

Continue growing in your relationship with God by regularly challenging yourself to trust His guidance in new areas, rely on His strength for greater levels of obedience, and seek His wisdom for decisions that stretch your faith beyond what feels comfortable or natural. Spiritual growth happens when you step into situations that require more of His presence than you've previously experienced, creating opportunities for fresh encounters with His faithfulness.

Finally, maintain your knowing place by remembering that it's not a spiritual destination you reach once but a way of living that requires a daily choice to prioritize relationship with God above all other pursuits, to seek His presence above all other experiences, and to value His approval above all other opinions.

The intimacy with God you've discovered through this devotional is meant to be the beginning of a lifetime journey into ever-deeper relationship with His presence, not the completion of your spiritual development. Continue seeking, growing, and discovering new dimensions of His love and faithfulness as you live from **THE KNOWING PLACE** for the rest of your life.